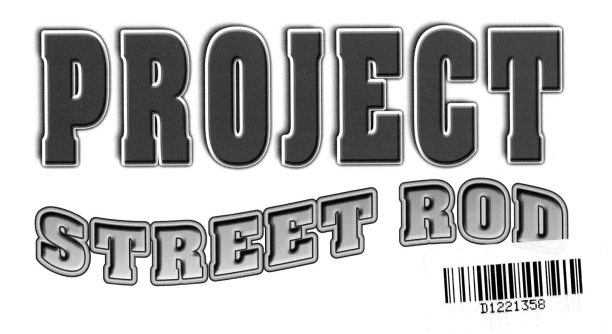

PROJECT STREET ROD

D1221358

The Step-by-Step Modification of a Vintage Car

From AUTO RESTORER® Magazine

By Larry Lyles

BOWTIE PRESS®

A Division of BowTie, Inc.
Laguna Hills, California

Barbara Kimmel, *Editor in Chief*
Nick Clemente, *Special Consultant*
Ted Kade, *Consulting Editor*
Kara Smith, *Production Supervisor*
Bill Jonas, *Layout Artist*
Indexed by Melody Englund

Library of Congress Cataloging-in-Publication Data

Lyles, Larry.
  Project street rod : the step-by-step restoration of a popular vintage car / by Larry Lyles.
      p. cm.
  "From Auto restorer magazine."
  ISBN 978-1-933958-39-2
  1. Hot rods—United States—Design and construction. 2. Ford automobile—Customizing. 3. Ford automobile—Conservation and restoration. I. Title.

  TL236.3.L95 2008
  629.2'3—dc22

                              2008014255

BowTie Press®
A Division of BowTie, Inc.
23172 Plaza Pointe Dr., Ste. 230
Laguna Hills, California 92653

Printed and bound in Singapore
15 14 13 12 11 10 09   1 2 3 4 5 6 7 8 9 10

Contents

Acknowledgments

I would like to thank the people who put a lot of time and effort into the rebirth of this car. Without their help, this project might never have been completed: Ted Kade, editor, *Auto Restorer Magazine*, whose expertise with words breathed life into the articles this book was taken from; John Sloane and Joe Richardson, the Eastwood Company, two guys who delivered on every promise made and then some; my wife, Pat; my son, Bryan; and the Biscuit, whose help, assistance, and enthusiasm keep me going.

Introduction

Had someone asked me as I began to put the finishing touches on the *Project Mustang* car if I planned to start another big project, I would have said "no way." I desperately needed a couple of days off to take care of a few nagging issues that were weighing heavily upon me, the weather was exceedingly hot, and starting a new project just wasn't what I had in mind.

My, how things can change so quickly. The rains came, the air cooled down, my battered body began to heal, and my apprentice, Bryan, found a 1946 Ford Business Coupe. But don't start laughing just yet. As you already know, my forte is 1960s muscle cars. I restore them, revamp them, retro them, and revive them. I don't do '46 Fords.

But then Bryan convinced me to take a walk around the '46 and give some thought to what could be done to the car. I liked the shape, if modified a little. I liked the interior room, if modified a little. I also liked the fact that someone else had already transplanted a Chevy 350 under the hood, although it, too, could stand to be modified a little. I was beginning to like what I saw.

I made a second trip around the car to kick the tires, then made up my mind that this 1946 Ford was going to get a new life, and I was going to eat my own words about not doing '46 Fords.

The catch was I had no desire to take this car apart and rebuild it back to original, the way I did in *Project Charger* and *Project Mustang*. What I had in mind would require a completely different mind-set on my part.

My thought was to take this aging vintage ride, which even in its prime was not much more than a means for moving from point A to point B, and upscale it into something very nice. Don't get the idea I'm about to hack apart a perfectly good original vintage ride and change it into something different. This car sat in the weeds far too many years to even consider that option. What the mice didn't eat the sun baked into crumbs. All I have now is a bullet-riddled hull in need of a lot of TLC and a whole host of modifications designed to transform this car into one heck of a nice ride.

I'm not looking for maximum horsepower, radical looks, or big tires. My goal is to transform this '46 Ford into something that looks nice, is very dependable, and is decked out with many of the modern-day trappings my wife would insist are necessities, not accessories.

What does that mean? In this case it means taking the car down to the bare frame and starting over using the latest in automotive ride, handling, and performance technology to rebuild it. In the end, what you will see from the outside is a somewhat modified '46 Ford; but on the inside, it will have all the modern accoutrements necessary to bring this car up to today's driving and handling standards.

In some parts of the country, this type of work, in which a car that in many cases is unsafe to drive at 50 mph is taken and modified to be safe to drive at any speed desired, is referred to as "resto-mod." In the sticks where I come from, we simply call it making the car "wife approved."

CHAPTER 1

GETTING STARTED

ake a look in photo 1 at where this car came from. The previous owner informed me he had spent several hours cutting down heavy brush and small trees just to reach the car. Once access to the car was gained, he towed the car into the open where it could be photographed, loaded onto a trailer, and transported to his garage. That was a few years ago, and I assure you that in the meantime the overall condition of the car wasn't drastically improved upon.

A NICE CAR IT ISN'T

The '46 was a bomb, to say the least. A lot of vital parts were missing, and the ones that were there had been used for target practice. I'm not stepping out on a limb when I say this car probably would have never seen pavement again; and if by some fluke it had, it would have been a risk to everyone within 100 yards of it. But that's no longer true. I'll be taking this aging hull of a car apart and making a lot of modifications designed to bring this car back to something that will handle and drive like a dream.

How am I going to do that? Let's move this bomb of a '46 into the shop and start by defusing it.

The previous owner was kind enough to remove all of the front sheet metal, which for the time being has been piled in a corner of the shop. That has left everything forward of the firewall exposed enough to give me a better look at what I have (photo 2).

REPLACING THE SUSPENSION

What I see I really don't like. The front I-beam axle setup may have been a good suspension system in its day, but it can't hold a candle to the modern IFS (independent front suspension) units available today (photo 3). Nor am I thrilled with the drum brake system or the manual steering setup. What this car needs is a good SLA (short arm, long arm) suspension system coupled with a set of disc brakes and rack and pinion steering.

The good news is that I can purchase an off-the-shelf IFS unit that will come already equipped with disc brakes and rack and pinion steering. That will let me rip out the

old front I-beam axle setup, then weld in the new IFS unit, and end up with a state-of-the-art front suspension. The bad news is that most off-the-shelf IFS units won't simply drop into place under the '46. To get one to fit, I'll need to make some modifications to the frame. As I move deeper into this project, I'll go through the entire process of modifying the frame to accept such a unit.

PHOTO 1: Parked in the weeds for many years, it took the previous owner two days to extract the car and save it from the "rust worms."

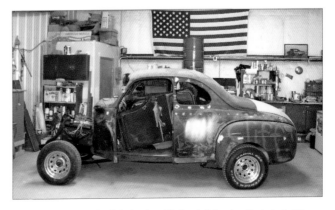

PHOTO 2: With the '46 finally in the shop, it is time to take a hard look at what I have.

THE ENGINE AND TRANSMISSION NEED ATTENTION

Looking at the engine the previous owner had already installed in the car, I know I have a very solid Chevy 350 bolted to a pretty common 350 automatic transmission (photo 4). Depending on the budget, I hope to be making some internal changes to the engine to boost its output as well as making a few cosmetic changes designed to dress up this engine. I'll also be thinking about giving the carburetor the toss, in favor of something a little more high tech and user friendly to the driver, such as a multiport fuel injection system from Affordable Fuel Injection. I've yet to teach Bryan the subtle nuances of starting a cold engine with a 650 Edelbrock mounted on it. I don't think the term *pump it* computes to a younger generation brought up on fuel-injected grocery haulers.

Anyway, as far as the transmission goes, overdrive would be nice, but sometimes you just have to "run what you brung." That doesn't mean this transmission is a slouch; GM thought enough of it to plant it under a few million Chevrolets. As long as I send it out for a once-over at the transmission shop, it should serve this project quite well for a number of years.

Crawling under the car to check the clearance between the transmission and the X-member, I can see that the frame will require some extensive modifications in this area also. The transmission is bumping the X-member on the right side and has less than a ¼-inch clearance on the left side. In an ideal world, I'd like to see at least a ½-inch clearance all around the transmission. That means I'll be modifying the X-member to gain that desired clearance.

TOP AND BOTTOM METAL WORK

Working my way farther back, I'm finding a lot of rust in the passenger compartment floor pan area that will have to be dealt with, plus a massively bubbled roof that is just begging for some attention. The floor pans are an easy enough fix. I'll simply cut them out and replace them with new pans fabricated here in the shop. The bubbled roof is going to present more of a challenge (photo 5). It will have to be chopped.

But then, that is an art in itself. If you have ever wandered through the local car shows admiring all of the painted iron on display, I'm sure you have noticed at least one ride with the windshield so narrow you can't help but wonder how the driver can see where he is going. That's a huge problem I want to avoid when it comes time to chop this top. I'm not fond of massive tops, but I am fond of seeing where I'm going.

The flip side to the overly chopped top is the chop that leaves the casual observer wondering if the top has been chopped at all. I don't want to spend the amount of time and money required to do a first-class top chop and then in the end realize I had needed to remove another inch of metal to really make this ride look right. To get it

PHOTO 3: I-beam front suspension with its drum brake setup has got to go. I'll replace everything here with something much better.

PHOTO 4: The Chevy 350 is a good start toward making this car really purr. It needs a little dressing up, but that's for later.

> **TIP**
>
> *A good way to keep your pants clean when going under a vehicle is to purchase a mechanic's creeper. This board on wheels keeps you off of the cold floor and makes negotiating the tight clearance between car and floor much easier.*

right, I'll use an old school trick combined with new-school technology to determine the correct amount of chop the roof panel should have.

I'll dispense with going into the details of how this chop will be accomplished until later. Instead, I'll explain the odd-looking car in photo 6. The lines across the door opening were created using masking tape. The strips of tape are spaced ¾ of an inch apart. That will allow me to take a photo of the car, blow it up to a larger size, then cut and crop it along the different tape lines until I determine how much chop is enough to make this car look the way I want it to look. I'll tack my cut and cropped shot of the car to the shop wall to serve as a reference guide as I work. I know, Photoshop can do that on the computer, but it can't blow up the picture enough for an old goat like me to get a real good look at it. I'm old school in that regard and proud of it.

Moving on toward the back of the car, the trunk floor pan is almost as rusty as the passenger compartment floor pan. Replacing it won't pose a serious problem until I toss into the mix the need to replace the fuel tank. I'm not thrilled with the fender-mounted fuel filler neck, so I will be making changes in that area also.

Under the rear floor pan is a GM-type rear axle assembly that had been removed from something with a rear coil spring suspension and modified to accept leaf springs. Nothing about this setup is acceptable to me, so the only alternative is to remove everything under here and start over. I just happen to have a Ford 8.8 rear axle complete with disc brakes and a factory four bar–type suspension that should be an easy fit.

IMPROVING INTERIOR COMFORT

Moving back to the passenger compartment, I know from having helped hot-rod a few cars over my career that there are two basic areas of concern located between the firewall and trunk compartment. The first is the dash area. Leg room can become a premium when trying to tuck air conditioning, stereo equipment, and a variety of gauges into an already confined space. This will take some careful thought and consideration as to how to proceed.

The other concern is the back seat. Did I say back seat? Yes, I did. The '46 may have begun life as a business coupe, void of a back seat, but it has more than enough room to accommodate a rear seat. It won't have the space

PHOTO 5: From this angle, you can almost get a feel for how the roof will look once it has been chopped. From any other angle, the roof is one huge bubble.

PHOTO 6: The first step in the old-school process of chopping a top is to lay reference lines on the car to be used later to determine the exact amount of chop this car will receive.

of a limo, but it should have ample room to stuff a grandkid or two into the car to make the day's outing a little more family friendly.

TIME FOR A WISH LIST

Normally, I would bring out the camera and note pad and start a master list as I begin to take this car apart. However, there isn't a lot to be taken apart on this car, and most of what I will be taking apart will not be put back on the car anyway. I think the best course of action is to start by compiling a wish list of desired changes, then venture onto the Internet in search of parts and parts catalogs. That will help me construct a budget for this project as well as help establish a sequence of steps for rebuilding this car.

NOTES

NOTES

CHAPTER 2

DISASSEMBLY AND MEASUREMENTS

Whenever I begin a new project, the first thing I do is position the car in the shop and elevate it on jack stands. That places the vehicle at a comfortable working height and also affords me ample room when I need to go underneath the vehicle to remove all those road-grime-coated parts. This project will be approached a little differently.

For the time being, the wheels will stay on the car and the car will stay on the floor. That's because I have a number of modifications I want to make to the frame under this car, and the best way to access the frame to accomplish those modifications is to remove the body. To do that, I'll use an engine hoist to lift the body straight up, then I'll roll the chassis out from underneath. The body will be sent out for media blasting to get rid of the rust while I concentrate on modifying the frame. How do I maneuver a bulky car body around the shop? I have a steel cart measuring roughly 4 x 6 feet with rollers under it (photo 1). It is strong enough to support almost anything I place on it.

SOME CHASSIS ANALYSIS

With the body off of the car, three things jump out at me as I study the chassis. First, the front suspension is an I-beam-style axle, and it has got to go. I-beam axles may look good under a Bucket T or a '32 Ford, but this type of suspension is never going to give me the quality of ride or degree of handling I'm looking for with this project (photo 2).

Second, the transplanted GM rear axle assembly and its accompanying leaf spring suspension also must go (photo 3). I have no kick against GM products or leaf spring rear suspensions, it is just that I have a very nice Ford 8.8 rear end complete with a factory four-bar suspension that not only will give this car a smooth ride but also will give me some options when it comes to determining the final riding height of the car.

Third, now that I have the body off of the frame and a better view of the center X-member, I can see some

PHOTO 1: The body is placed on a steel cart to allow me to move it around the shop as needed.

PHOTO 2: This I-beam axle and drum brake setup may have been state of the art in 1946, but to meet today's standards it has to go.

PHOTO 3: The GM rear axle came from a car with a coil spring suspension. It was converted to leaf springs, and now I'm converting it to dust gatherer.

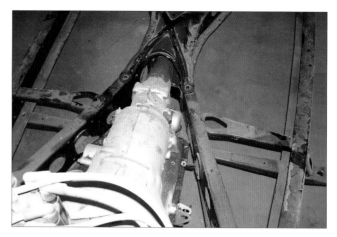

PHOTO 4: The lack of clearance around the transmission makes this installation unacceptable. I'll have to make some modifications to this part of the frame.

hacking and chopping has already taken place to get the automatic transmission to fit. I use the word *fit* loosely, as this installation is anything but acceptable (photo 4). The transmission is bumping the frame on the right side and doesn't offer much more room on the left. I knew these were areas of concern coming into the project, so all that is left for me to do now is go to work and fix them.

THE DISASSEMBLY BEGINS

I start by placing the chassis on jack stands so I can remove the wheels and gain a little more working room. Next, I remove the engine and transmission. I'd like to hang the engine on an engine stand and send the transmission out for a rebuild, but I'll need both units a little later to help reconfigure the engine and transmission mounts. So for now, I leave the transmission attached to the engine and store them in the corner where hopefully they will be out of the way until I need them.

The next piece to go is the GM rear end. A few bolts and the unit will drop right out. I'm not going to concern myself with marking the rear axle centerline on the frame to help position the new axle because the previous owner installed this rear axle, and I can't be sure he installed it to the correct dimensions in the first place. To determine the correct rear axle centerline, I have access to a set of original 1946 Ford frame dimensions that will at least give me a place to start.

The front I-beam axle is a different story. Up here, the old suspension is basically stock, so before any of these parts are removed, I'll mark a reference point on the frame to help define where the front axle centerline should be located. I'll also take a measurement from the axle to a point roughly 4 feet back on the frame that

will help me when I'm ready to install the new front suspension.

The reference point for the axle centerline is found by laying a straightedge across the frame from center to center of both axle kingpins and marking the centerline on the top of the frame. I won't use this mark as the ultimate guide to positioning the new front suspension within the frame, but it will serve as a base reference point later when I install the new front suspension cross member.

The other measurement I need is from the axle centerline mark on the frame back to a hole in the top of the frame located just behind the front body mounts. That measurement is 52 inches. With these two specifications noted and marked, I can unbolt the old front suspension and remove it as a complete unit.

DOWN TO THE BARE BONES

With the '46 stripped down to the bare frame, my next step is to determine an approximate final curb height for the car. How am I going to manage that with no suspension under the car? Actually, it won't be that difficult. Since I'll be modifying the frame to accept new suspension components, I can control the position of those components by the way I install them on the frame. That begins by determining the amount of ground clearance I'll ultimately want under the car. I'll use the body mount perches riveted to the sides of the frame as measuring points and level the frame at 14 inches (photo 5). This is an arbitrary number and may change as I move deeper into the project, but for now it gives me a good place to start.

The plan also calls for giving this car a few degrees of front-end rake when finished. That means the front of the car will sit slightly lower than the rear, so leveling the car at 14 inches will actually end up giving me a car that sits roughly 16–18 inches from floor level at the rear and roughly 10–12 inches from floor level at the front when completed. Sound confusing? It does. But trust me, everything will work out. I just need the frame to sit dead level for now to ensure that every modification I make to the frame ends up level to the frame and not installed crooked or leaning off toward the back forty. What did I use to level the frame? In this case, a long carpenter's level isn't of much use since the frame has several dips and bumps along its length. Instead, I opted for a short, 12-inch-long level I could place at various points along the frame, both lengthwise and crosswise, to get it level. Having a large supply of paint stir sticks also helps, as they can act as shims where needed between the jack stands and frame.

Now I can move my replacement Ford 8.8 rear axle into position under the car. I use three jack stands to support the unit, placing a stand just inboard of each brake flange and another under the pinion yoke to support the front of the axle.

I set the rear axle centerline height at 14½ inches just because my jack stands have a lock at that exact point. If the jack stands had locked at 14 or 15 inches, either would have worked just as well (photo 6).

To be sure the axle is positioned squarely within the fame as well as positioned correctly lengthwise, I referred to the set of 1946 Ford frame dimensions mentioned earlier and place the 8.8 axle at 32¼ inches forward of the rearmost tip of the frame when measuring from the axle centerline to the end of the frame.

To determine the square placement of the axle assembly within the frame, I take cross measurements between the axle and the frame from side to side. When those measurements are equal, I know the axle is positioned squarely within the frame (photo 7).

With the axle assembly positioned correctly, I need to do two more things. First, I want to level the pinion yoke and take a measurement from the center of the yoke to the floor, in this case 12½ inches. I file this measurement away until the engine and transmission are ready to be installed.

After that, I need to elevate the pinion and set it at 3 degrees positive. This is an absolutely critical step, as 3 degrees positive is the pinion angle determined by car manufacturers and hot rod builders many years ago to be the optimum angle for installing and mounting any rear axle assembly. How come? Consider how difficult it is to keep a

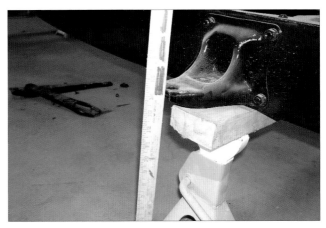

PHOTO 5: A yardstick is used to help set the riding height of the car by measuring the distance from the floor to the body mount, in this case, 14 inches.

PHOTO 6: Sticking with my proposed riding height of 14 inches, the rear axle centerline is set to 14½ inches. The extra ½ inch is to compensate for the jack stands and will not affect the actual riding height when the car is completed.

PHOTO 7: Taking cross measurements is a vital part of centering the rear axle within the frame.

double-hinged tube balanced and rotating in a perfectly straight line when spun. Add an upward bias to the hinges to eliminate the straight line effect, and suddenly the tube becomes very easy to balance and spin. In this case, that tube is the driveshaft.

To find the 3 degrees positive angle, I place a magnetic protractor on top of the pinion yoke and shim the yoke up by adding paint stir sticks between the yoke and the jack stand until the magnetic protractor reads 3 degrees positive (photo 8). I'll get deeper into the need for the level pinion measurement as well as the role this 3-degree placement plays in this build once I'm ready to install the engine and transmission. For now, I need to concentrate on mounting this axle to the frame.

SELECTING A SUSPENSION SYSTEM

When it comes to mounting and supporting a rear axle assembly, the average car builder has a variety of suspension systems from which to choose. They range from the common everyday suspensions found under factory-built cars to the more exotic systems designed and produced through the racing and street rod building industries.

The most common rear suspensions found are the same types of rear suspensions the auto makers have been using for years: the leaf spring and coil spring suspensions. The basic difference between these two suspensions has to do with the axle. The leaf spring suspension not only supports the rear axle as it dampens the effects of the road, it also provides the means by which the axle is mounted to the vehicle. The coil spring suspension also supports the vehicle and provides a dampening effect for

PHOTO 8: The pinion angle is set to 3 degrees positive in order to give the axle housing a slight upward bias.

the bumps on the road, but the axle itself is secured to the vehicle by a set of four bars, or four mounting arms, that hold the axle in place while allowing it to move up and down within the frame.

As previously mentioned, the rear suspension I removed from this car used leaf springs to support the axle assembly and in any other situation would have been an adequate suspension. However, replacing the unit with the Ford 8.8 rear axle instantly transforms this project car into a vehicle equipped with four wheel disc brakes. Not a bad trade-off.

If there is a downside here it is that the Ford unit was designed as a coil spring, four mounting arm–type suspension. That means more work installing the unit, but it also means I can make some changes and toss the coil springs in favor of adjustable coil-over shocks.

Adjustable coil-over shocks offer two things I might not otherwise have. First, adjustable coil-over shocks will allow me to adjust the final riding height of the car by varying the amount of compression applied to the coil springs. Second, if I don't like the ride the coil-over shocks are giving me, I can easily swap out the coils to give the car a stiffer ride or, if desired, a softer ride.

But there is nothing to bolt this rear axle to. That's why every decent-size city has a metal mart. I'll make a visit to my local mart and purchase a 10 foot length of 2 x 2–inch square steel tubing (this is industry jargon) and an even dozen $\frac{1}{8}$-inch-thick steel plates measuring 4 x 6 inches. I'll use the tubing to construct the necessary mounting brackets and the steel plates to construct mounting boxes to accept the four axle mounting arms.

Photo 9 shows one of the lower mounting brackets fabricated from the 2 x 2–inch square tubing. The triangular shape gives the bracket plenty of strength and provides adequate area to weld the unit to the frame.

To mount these brackets, one on the right and one on the left, I cut square openings inside the frame rails to allow the brackets to slide into the rails, where they can be welded into place (photo 10). Notice the clamps. For the time

PHOTO 9: One of the lower mounting brackets fabricated from the 2 x 2-inch square tubing.

PHOTO 10: Before welding, the entire rear axle mounting system is mocked up and clamped into place.

being, nothing has been welded. I save the welding until I have everything fitting the way I want them to fit.

To attach the upper axle mounting arms to the frame, I cut square holes in both sides of the frame and slide a length of 2 x 2 square tubing through the frame and extend it out ¼ inch on both sides. This allows me to weld the tubing to the frame on the outside of the rail as opposed to cutting access holes inside the frame rail to facilitate welding.

Next, I use the 4 x 6 steel plates to form gussets to attach the mounting arms to the square tubing. Once the mounts are secured, I finish this installation by capping the ends of the square tubing with scraps from the ⅛-inch steel plate.

To double-check my work, I again measure the positioning of the axle within the frame to be sure everything remained square and in good alignment. I also use a floor jack to move the axle up and down to be sure nothing is binding and that I have smooth operation everywhere. When I'm sure everything is in place, I finish welding all of the brackets and grind each weld smooth.

MOUNTING THE SHOCKS

With the axle solidly in place, my next step is to mount the coil-over shocks. The actual up-and-down travel of these shocks is 5 inches. That means with the frame and the rear axle sitting at the assumed riding height of the car, I need to mount the shocks so that they will have 2½ inches of travel up and 2½ inches of travel down.

The upward travel, or extension travel, of the shock isn't so critical because this movement places virtually no stress on the shock; it merely extends its full length and stops. At that point, the rear wheel lifts and in an extreme case may even lift off of the ground.

The downward travel, or compression travel, of the shock is more critical because this movement places a lot of stress on the shock as it attempts to compress the oil or gas inside the shock. This compression action, if pushed to an extreme, can result in the shock rupturing and rendering it useless. To prevent the shock from overcompressing, I need to install rubber cushions between the axle unit and the frame. These snubbers, as they are called, stop the upward travel of the axle, thereby preventing the shock from being overcompressed.

I elected to use rubber lower control arm stops found on the 1968 Mustang and mounted each one to a bracket made of 2 x 2 square tubing extended downward from the frame (photo 11). When the axle is forced upward, it will bump into the snubber and stop, thereby saving my shock.

The snubber brackets are 6 inches long, with each snubber extending that length by 1 inch. That gives me an upward axle travel from the neutral position of 2¼ inches, but that is still enough to provide this car with a smooth, secure ride.

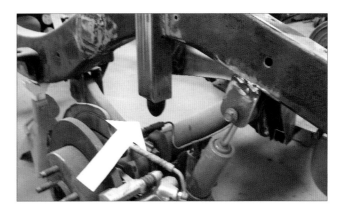

PHOTO 11: This bracket holds the rubber axle stop designed to prevent the coil-over shock from bottoming out and being damaged.

NOTES

NOTES

CHAPTER 3

INSTALLING THE
FRONT SUSPENSION

There is good news when it comes to removing an old front suspension and replacing it with a more modern suspension. The aftermarket street rod industry has had many years to design and produce replacement units that far exceed the performance of the older original suspensions.

The bad news is that if the installation of the new suspension isn't done correctly, the vehicle being modified may actually drive and handle worse than it did with the vintage front suspension. The lesson here is, if you are considering such an undertaking, buying new parts doesn't guarantee a job well done. For that you will need to gather all the information you can find concerning how a suspension works before ever turning a bolt on the old suspension to remove it. Where do you find such information? This book is a good place to start. After that, visit the local front end alignment store, where you can talk to the tech about what you are doing. His time costs money. Pay him.

THE PROJECT'S NEW SUSPENSION

The front suspension I've chosen for this project is known as an IFS, or independent front suspension. It is also known as the Mustang II front suspension because it is basically an improved version of the original Mustang II front suspension. In the restoration world, this front end is also known as an SLA suspension, or short arm, long arm suspension. Short arm means the upper control arm is shorter than the lower control arm, as shown in photo 1. OK, I know this is going to come up, so here goes. The upper control arm is shorter because this setup acts to keep more of the tire on the road at all times, especially when cornering, and that greatly improves upon the handling qualities of the vehicle.

This type of replacement front suspension consists of three main components: a front cross member, shown already welded into place on the frame in photo 2, and the right and left upper control arm mounting brackets, at this point only tack welded to the frame.

Photo 2 shows how the front cross member is positioned within the frame and how the upper control arm brackets are positioned on top of the frame rail, and it

PHOTO 1: A bird's-eye view of an SLA front end. Notice how much shorter the upper control arm is than the lower control arm.

PHOTO 2: This is a finished view of the new cross member installation. Notice the new round tube at the front of the frame put there for cosmetic reasons, the dogleg created just aft of the cross member when the frame was narrowed, the new cross member itself, the upper control arm mounting plates, and, finally, the motor mount brackets. Phew! No wonder this took forever!

also points out a lot of other things that are going on at the same time.

For instance, the frame has been narrowed to fit the new front cross member, the engine mounts have been tack welded into place, and the front tip of the frame has been cosmetically dressed out with a round steel tube. These are all steps that must be considered before ever opening the toolbox to start building a new front suspension.

These parts may be the guts of the new suspension, but in the overall scheme of things they represent only three pieces in a long list of parts that are needed to complete the transformation. Let's take a look at the rest of the components that make up this IFS unit, and then I'll explain some of the basics that make the IFS unit such a good choice when you are updating an older vehicle with a modern front suspension.

THOSE CUSTOM CONTROL ARMS

If you have ever had a disassembled front suspension, all of the parts in photo 3 will look familiar. With the exception of the control arms, which are custom-made tubular units, all of these pieces can be purchased off the shelf at the local automotive parts store. These are all Ford or Ford-compatible components and are as follows: disc brake rotors, disc brake calipers, spindles, coil springs, shock absorbers, and a power rack and pinion steering unit.

Did I say power steering? Yes I did. Recall that I said at the beginning of this project the goal would be to

bring this car up to today's standards and make it wife approved. Power steering is one of those requirements.

As for the custom tubular control arms, I elected to go with these parts to ensure that the front suspension on this car wouldn't have that "borrowed from the salvage yard" look. Less expensive stamped-control arms are available, and they work just fine. Their only knock is that they look a little too factory to suit my taste.

FITTING THE NEW CROSS MEMBER

Referring back to photo 2, it is obvious that changes had been made to the frame to accommodate the installation of this suspension. To start, I had removed the bulky original cross member that supported the old front suspension as well as the smaller forward cross member located at the front tip of the frame. Both pieces had to go to narrow the frame to accept the new cross member. Why didn't I just order a cross member that would fit my existing frame? I could have, but it would have taken several more weeks and hundreds more dollars to have the piece custom fabricated. Purchasing an off-the-shelf unit not only saved me a few bucks, it also allowed me to stay on schedule. And it affords me the opportunity to demonstrate how to narrow a frame correctly.

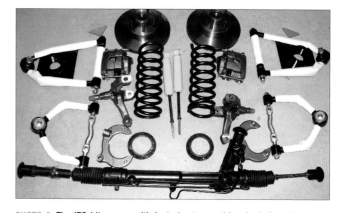

PHOTO 3: The IFS kit comes with just about everything, including the control arms, spindles, springs, shocks, brake rotors, brake calipers, and a power rack and pinion steering unit.

SOME NIPPING AND TUCKING

The first step to narrowing any portion of a frame is to determine how much the frame needs to be narrowed. In this case, the original frame measured 26 inches wide at the old cross member location when measured from inside edge to inside edge of each frame rail. While I was at it, I also measured the width of the frame at the front tip. This point measured 29 inches wide from outside edge to outside edge. I'll explain the need for this measurement later.

The replacement cross member measures 23 inches wide at the support flanges, where it welds to the inside of the frame rails. That's a difference of 3 inches between the width of my new cross member where it mounts to the frame and the existing frame rails. This difference is the reason for the need to narrow the frame.

Now that I know the frame must be narrowed by a total of 3 inches to fit my new cross member, I divide that number in half to determine how much to narrow each rail: 1½ inches.

ASSESSING THE RAILS

Making an observation of the frame rails before making any cuts tells me this frame is basically straight from just behind the old cross member forward to the front tip of the frame. That also tells me that any cuts I make should be made behind where the old cross member mounted and in the area where the frame begins to flare out as it widens and moves under the body of the car. This is preferable in that it lets me make my cuts and bends where anyone looking at the frame would expect to see bends and curves. It is the perfect hiding place.

MAKING THE FRAME PIE CUTS

Working with one rail at a time, my first step is to determine exactly where on the rail to make my cuts. I'll start with the right rail. This isn't rocket science, so I just eye-ball the rail and pick my points. I make my first cut 18 inches back from the forward tip of the frame and the second cut 25 inches back.

Next, I make two full-scale templates of the rail area to be narrowed, one depicting the rail before being narrowed, the other depicting the narrowed frame using the proposed cut line points to make the bend in the rail. For clarification, I darken the proposed area of bend on both templates as shown in photo 4.

In the photo, the proposed areas of bend on the template were cut at 90 degrees. If I lay the protractor over the darkened areas and align it to the 90-degree cuts, it automatically gives me the precise angle to make my pie cuts in the frame rail in order to make the bends. That angle on both cuts is 10 degrees.

What is all this pie cut business? To bend the rail, I need to take a small wedge-shaped slice, or pie cut, out of the rail. This creates a gap in the sidewall of the rail so that when the rail is bent, the gap will close. Photo 5 offers a good view of how this wedge will be removed from the frame.

PHOTO 4: These templates depict the shape of the rail both before and after being narrowed. Notice the use of the protractor to determine the cut angles.

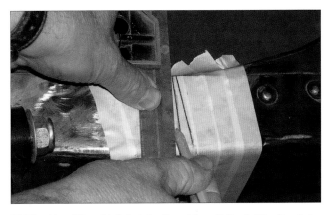

PHOTO 5: I taped the rail to help define the cut lines. Notice that the piece being removed resembles a wedge of pie, thus the name *pie cut.*

Since I'll be bending the rail inboard at the rearmost cut, I want to take my wedge from the inside of the rail. I'll use a reciprocating saw with an 8-inch metal cutting blade and remove my 10-degree wedge from the inner rail, allowing the cuts to taper to a point as they reach the outer wall of the rail.

For the second cut, I'll bend the forward portion of the rail outboard. That means the pie cut will be made on the outside of the frame, and it will also be 10 degrees wide.

With both cuts made, all of the strength of the frame rail is gone, and it will bend quite easily. To control each bend, I use a ratcheting cable puller that is attached to the opposite side of the frame and to a point between the two cuts to pull the rail inboard until the rearmost pie cut closes.

With the ratcheting cable puller holding the rail bent into place, I use a hydraulic ram placed between the front tips of the frame to push the forward section of the frame back out until the second pie cut closes (photo 6). The rail now has a dogleg bend just aft of the position where the old cross member was located, with the front section of the rail being once again straight and parallel with the

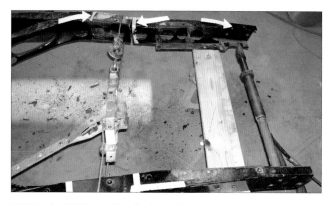

PHOTO 6: A ratcheting cable puller is used to bend the rail inboard at the rearmost cut, while a hydraulic ram is used to push the front section of the rail back out straight. I'll know the rail is bent correctly when the pie cuts close.

PHOTO 7: The new cross member is positioned within the frame and leveled.

opposite, uncut rail. I'll take measurements from the same points I used earlier to determine the precut width of the frame, and with any luck my new measurements will read 24½ inches and 27½ inches, respectively, exactly 1½ inches narrower than before.

This is a time-consuming process, and the old adage of measuring two times, three times, and a fourth time if necessary is very good advice. When the rail is perfect, I tack weld both pie cuts, then repeat the entire operation on the other rail.

Once both rails have been cut, bent, and tack welded into place, it is time to once again check my measurements. Remember the 29-inch measurement across the front tip of the frame? This measurement must now read 26 inches. If it does, the frame is perfect, and the measurement at the cross member should read 23 inches. If it doesn't, I must take frame cross measurements to see which rail is out of alignment.

I start by measuring from the first cut on the right rail to the tip of the left rail. That measurement must be 32 inches. If it isn't, the rail must be moved either inboard or outboard, depending on the measurement, to achieve the 32-inch reading. When both rail cross measurements equal 32 inches, the cross member measurement reads 23 inches, and the front tip reads 26 inches, it is time for the cross member.

INSTALLING THE FRONT CROSS MEMBER

Because of my precise measuring, the new front cross member will be a snug fit between the two rails. I use a floor jack to push the front cross member up into place, then leave the jack there as a support while I again take measurements.

If you recall, I took some preliminary measurements of the old front suspension before removing it. One of those measurements was taken from the front axle centerline to a hole in the top of the frame 52 inches back. I again measure from that hole forward and re-mark my axle centerline on both rails at 52 inches, using a long straightedge laid across the width of the frame. This will be the centerline for the new cross member. Once centered on the new axle centerline, the cross member is first leveled, then tack welded into place (photo 7). Now the real work of building this suspension can begin.

THE BUILDUP

With the front cross member tack welded into place, I want to mock up the left side of the suspension minus the coil spring and shock absorber. Remember, I'm only tack welding things together for now; adding the spring would be dangerous and at this point unnecessary.

I start by clamping the upper control arm mounting plate to the top of the frame rail directly above the new front cross member, then bolt on the upper and lower control arms and the spindle. These are critical parts to setting the C and C of this suspension. What are C and C? Glad you asked.

C AND C: CAMBER AND CASTER

If this car ever hopes to roll down the road straight and true, I have to get the camber and caster alignment points perfect. To do that, I really need to know what camber and caster are and how each one will affect the handling of this ride.

The basic definition of camber is "the inward or outward tilt of the wheel when viewed from the front of the vehicle." Here is an example: If a vertical line were drawn through the center of the wheel, it would be said to exhibit 0 degree camber. But if the wheel leaned inboard toward the engine from that same vertical line, the wheel would exhibit negative camber. On the other hand, if the wheel leaned outboard from that same vertical line, the wheel would exhibit positive camber. Improperly set camber causes excessive tire wear and allows the vehicle to wander all over the road.

Caster is defined as a "vertical line drawn from the ground up through the center of both the upper and the lower ball joints when viewed from the side of the car." The vertical alignment of both ball joints means the vehicle exhibits 0 degree caster. Improperly set caster may cause a nonreturn of the wheel after a turn, vehicle drift, or a pull to one side.

Ask any front suspension specialist, and he will tell you a positive degree setting on both the camber and caster is a must. So with that thought in mind, the first thing I do is support the lower control arm by placing a jack stand under the arm, then level it using paint stir sticks as shims. This leveling action places the suspension at the assumed normal ride height of the car.

Next, I place the magnetic protractor vertically on the flat of the spindle and check for positive camber (photo 8). With the upper control arm clamped into place at the full inboard position on the mounting panel, my reading is 2 degrees negative camber. That's a good thing. It means I've built into this front end a small amount of negative camber and a maximum 12 degrees positive camber, gained by moving the upper control arm full outboard. In a world where 1 to 2 degrees positive camber is ideal, everything is looking great.

To determine my caster setting, I place a 24-inch carpenter's square just in front of the ball joints and measure the distance from the square to each ball joint (photo 9). In this case, the distance from the lower ball joint measures 3 inches, and the distance from the upper ball joint measures 3 1/16 inches. That's perfect. My front end exhibits 2 degrees negative camber with plenty of positive degree adjustment, and my caster setting reads roughly 0.5 degree positive caster with plenty of positive degree adjustment available.

PHOTO 8: Notice that the upper control arm mount is only clamped into place. This allows me to move the mount if necessary to gain a positive degree reading on the magnetic protractor attached to the spindle.

PHOTO 9: With the upper control arm held full inboard, a measurement is taken at both ball joints to ensure their vertical alignment.

Had this measurement been, for example, 3 inches on the lower ball joint and 2½ inches on the upper ball joint, I would have needed to move the upper control arm mounting panel back until the upper ball joint measurement read a minimum of 3 inches.

Now I can tack weld the left upper control arm mounting panel to the frame and repeat this exercise on the right side.

SOME STEERING CHECKS

The only things left to verify up here is the placement of the rack and pinion steering assembly and the spindle to rear axle alignment. I start with the rack and pinion steering assembly. All I'm looking for here is to be certain the tie-rod ends bend slightly downward and backward when mounted to the spindles. This will eliminate any chance of bump steer caused by the tie-rod ends having a forward bias. Any necessary adjustments can be made by adding shims where the rack mounts to the frame.

To check the spindle to rear axle alignment, I attach a string at the center point of the rear axle and extend that string forward through the center of the upper ball joint then beyond to intersect the center of the tie-rod mounting hole on the spindle, with the wheel pointing straight ahead. Also known as Ackermann, this setting is important, as it gives the front wheels the correct toe-out when making turns. If the string doesn't intersect both the ball joint and the tie-rod hole, an alignment problem exists somewhere within the installation of the new cross member. Bring out the tape measure and double-check everything. As a last resort, consult your front suspension technician with hat and money in hand.

Once I know everything is set correctly—verified by having measured, measured again, checked, and checked again—the suspension components can be disassembled. The cross member, upper control arm mounting panels, and wedge plates can then be welded solid and ground smooth.

I didn't mention installing the wedge plates? This triangular-shaped metal plate, referred to as a wedge plate, is included in the IFS kit and must be welded between the lower control arm mounting tube and the new cross member to prevent the control arm from flexing any time the car makes a hard turn (photo 10).

Worried about heat warpage during welding? That's a huge concern. The remedy is to pick a point to begin welding, then weld a short bead, roughly 1 inch long, then move to another area of the frame and weld another short bead. Granted, this takes a lot of time, but this method works to keep the heat evenly distributed over the entire area being welded, thereby reducing the chances of heat warping any part of the frame. If necessary, a damp cloth will help cool the metal between welds, and a die grinder with a ⁵⁄₁₆-inch-thick, 3-inch-diameter grinding wheel will make short work of smoothing the welds.

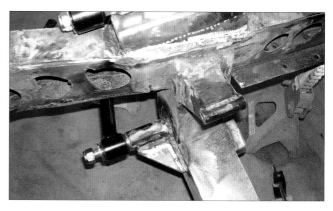

PHOTO 10: The triangular wedge plate must be welded to the lower control arm mounting tube for added reinforcement to prevent the control arm from flexing during a hard turn.

NOTES

CHAPTER 4

INSTALLING THE ENGINE

aving installed more than my share of engines and transmissions over my career as a car nut, this is an easy task to accomplish when all you have to do is drop the engine and transmission into the car and bolt the units into place. It is quite another story when there is nothing to which the units can be bolted, and in this case, even if I could bolt them down, the transmission would be bumping the X-member. That is where I am with this project. I have an engine bolted to a transmission, but what I don't have is a frame willing to accept them.

I could hang the engine and transmission over the frame, then when I think things look right weld in some mounts and hope for the best. I might even get away with that type of installation if the car were destined for the garage and not the road. But that isn't the case. This car is being built for the same purpose I have in mind for every other car I've built: to be driven. That's a shame, because now I have to get technical, and I never like to get too technical.

WEARING MY
TECHIE HAT FOR PHASE ONE

If you recall when I first started this project, one of the problem areas that stood out was the lack of clearance between the transmission and the X-member portion of the frame. The transmission was rubbing against the frame on the right side and had less than ½ inch of clearance on the left side. The only solution for this problem is to widen the front X-member rails to gain some space for the transmission.

To do that, I need to cut both X-member rails and bend them outward by 2 inches. Notice in photo 1 I've already made the first pie cut (left arrow) on the top flange of the left rail and marked the area near the X-member center brace (right arrow) for cutting the rail in half. Once the lower rail flange has been pie cut and the rail is cut in half at the brace, I can then bend the rail outward, and the end result will look like photo 2.

PHOTO 1: The left arrow points to the pie cut already made in the frame rail. The right arrow indicates where the rail will be cut through.

PHOTO 2: The two lower arrows indicate the pie cut locations on each rail. The upper left arrow points to the steel plate used to space the rail outward. The right upper arrow points to a bracket that had to be shortened to accommodate moving the rail, and the center arrow points to the new transmission mount.

So the question is, how did I get there from here? The first thing I did was to pick up pen and paper. This frame rail bending procedure is a very simple operation, but the cuts require specific angles so that when the rails are pushed out, the pie cuts will close and the reinforcing plates used to bridge the 2-inch gap at the X-member center braces will abut perfectly against the cut ends of the rails.

Photo 3 is a shop drawing I made to determine the precise angle for each cut. Notice on the drawing that the ends of the bent piece are drawn at 90 degrees. This helps me determine the angle of the cuts if I align the 90-degree mark on a protractor with the 90-degree drawing and measure the angle produced at that point. Notice the darkened wedge-shaped area near the left end of the bent piece as well. This is the area of overlap onto the uncut portion of the rail. When a protractor is laid over this darkened wedge and aligned with the 90-degree cut end on the drawing, the angle comes out to be 10 degrees. In this case, both the pie cuts and the through cut on the rail will be made at 90 degrees.

To transfer my 10-degree cut angle to the rail, I cover the rail with masking tape (photo 4), then use the protractor and a straightedge to lay out the cut lines. Nothing to it, but it does require a little precision.

The actual cuts will be made one rail at a time, starting with the right rail. That allows me to make the cuts using a reciprocating saw with a metal cutting blade attached. I use a hydraulic ram pressed against the left rail to push the right rail out until the 10-degree pie cuts close and the ⅛-inch-thick, 4 x 6–inch steel bridging plate perfectly spans the gap between the rail and the center brace. Once that is accomplished, the pie cuts and the bridging plate can be welded, and the widening process can be repeated on the left rail.

PHASE TWO

I actually have to start this phase with the driveshaft since this is the link between all that power up front and the rear axle, where that power is put to the pavement. To rephrase a phrase I heard somewhere, if the driveshaft ain't happy, ain't nothing about this drivetrain gonna be happy.

To make the driveshaft happy, I have to think about two factors: transverse vibration and torsional vibration. Transverse vibration is simple, so I'll talk about that first. Transverse vibration is a bending vibration and is the result of an improperly balanced or bent driveshaft. The cure? Never install a driveshaft without first having a qualified driveshaft shop check it out to be sure it is perfectly straight and balanced.

Torsional vibration is a twisting motion that usually occurs as a result of improper U-joint angles, and that is what all this is leading up to. Looking at an extreme case, if I installed the rear axle dead level 12 inches from the floor and the engine dead level 24 inches from the floor, the angle of the driveshaft between the two components would be severe, approaching 30 degrees, and torsional vibration at higher speeds would become a problem. It is this extreme type of driveshaft angle I need to prevent.

To do that, I start by lowering the engine and transmission toward the cross member until I reach a point where I think the engine should mount. Where is that? I want at least 1 inch of clearance between the oil pan and the cross member so when I reach that

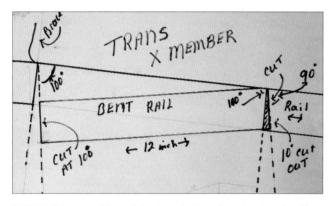

PHOTO 3: This may not be rocket science, but knowing where to cut and how much to cut saves a lot of headaches later on. Cutting the rail on paper first keeps me headed in the right direction.

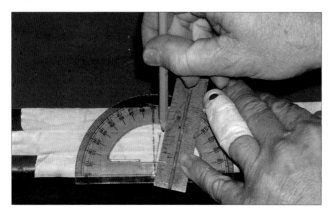

PHOTO 4: The information from the template is now transferred to the rail for cutting.

point, I'll stop. Now I take a measurement from the output shaft on the transmission to the floor. That reading is 15 inches.

With that done, I carefully shift the engine until the motor mounts bolted to the block are centered over the cross member. That's because the plan calls for welding the new motor mount brackets to the cross member. With the engine in position over the cross member and still suspended by the hoist, I need to give the engine 3 degrees backward, or negative, tilt using the magnetic protractor.

But here's the catch. Most carburetor intake manifolds have 3 degrees positive tilt built into them to compensate for the negative 3 degrees the engine should exhibit. That ensures that the carburetor sits level in the car. It also means that if the engine is setting level, the magnetic protractor, when placed on top of the carburetor mounting plate, will read 3 degrees positive tilt. To achieve the 3 degrees negative tilt I need for the engine, the magnetic protractor must read 0 degree (photo 5). I'll explain the need for this degree setting in a moment.

I also level the engine from side to side to make determining the length of the motor mount brackets a little easier (if the engine is level, both mounting brackets will automatically be the same length).

DETERMINING THE DRIVESHAFT ANGLE

It's time to screw the Techie hat down tight. Every time my brain shifts into overdrive, I can smell a clutch burning.

Recall in chapter 2 that I gave the rear axle assembly 3 degrees positive tilt during installation. If I extend a straight line forward from the center of the pinion shaft while exhibiting the same 3 degrees positive tilt as the rear axle, that line will slowly rise to intersect the transmission about 2½ inches below the center of the output shaft. If a straight line is drawn from the center of the transmission output shaft when exhibiting 3 degrees negative tilt back to the rear axle, that line will intersect the rear axle housing 2½ inches above the center of the pinion shaft. Now consider that both of these imaginary lines are parallel to each other and separated by 2½ inches. I have reached perfection.

Confusing, isn't it? Refer to photo 6.

Assume the left end of this bar is the engine and transmission and the right end is the rear axle assembly. Now assume the top surface of the bar is indicative of a line drawn straight through the crankshaft and transmission tail shaft, all the way back to the rear axle,

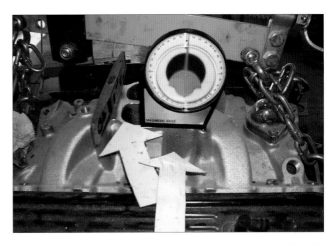

PHOTO 5: With the engine still on the hoist, it is first leveled side to side using the 12-inch level, and then it's given a 3-degree backward tilt using the magnetic protractor.

PHOTO 6: A visual example of how I set up the drivetrain to ensure that the driveshaft angle is less than 5 degrees.

and the bottom of the bar is indicative of a line drawn straight through the rear axle pinion shaft forward to the transmission tail shaft. It is easy to see these two lines are parallel to each other. That is what I'm looking for, the line drawn through the tail shaft to intersect the rear axle housing just above the pinion shaft, and the line drawn through the pinion shaft to intersect the transmission just below the tail shaft.

And now the clutch really begins to burn.

I know the measurement from the center of the tail shaft to the floor on this '46 Ford is 15 inches and the measurement from the center of the pinion shaft to the floor is 12½ inches. That's a difference of 2½ inches. Falling back on what little I learned in Calculus Approximation 303, I elevate the left jack stand in photo 6 until I get a measurement of 15 inches from the top of the bar to the floor, and I elevate the right jack stand until I get a measurement of 12½ inches from the top of the bar to the floor. This represents the centerline between the transmission and the rear axle pinion shaft.

What the heck am I doing? Long, long ago in a world filled with bent driveshafts and broken U-joints, someone discovered that a driveshaft operating at an angle of less than 3 degrees from true horizontal could be safely spun at rpms exceeding 5000, whereas driveshaft operating angles exceeding 6 degrees could be detrimental to a driveshaft spinning at less than 4000 rpm. My makeshift template in photo 6 gives me the operating angle of my driveshaft.

The verdict is? The magnetic protractor in photo 7 tells the tale. My driveshaft should have a normal ride angle of 2 degrees. That means this drive line should operate very smoothly and last almost forever.

PHOTO 7: Using my makeshift driveshaft template, I can determine the driveshaft angle using a magnetic protractor. In this case, the driveshaft angle is 2 degrees.

DETERMINING THE DRIVESHAFT LENGTH

But the driveshaft angle doesn't help much without an actual driveshaft to couple the transmission to the rear axle. This is a task I turn over to a qualified professional, as this driveshaft will have to be custom made. After all, I'm connecting a GM transmission to a Ford rear axle. It's like putting '58 Cadillac taillights in an '83 Honda Civic. It can be done, but only if you know what you are doing.

I know of two ways to determine the length of a new driveshaft. Both should be done with the full weight of the vehicle on the floor. That's not possible in this case, but I do have the entire chassis set up to simulate the correct riding height of the car. That should be close enough.

The first method calls for measuring from the end of the transmission output shaft to the center of the U-joint on the pinion shaft. That measurement is 53¼ inches. I also measure the distance the tail shaft housing extends beyond the output shaft, ½ inch. I'll give both of these measurements to the driveshaft shop along with the necessary transmission and rear axle information (makes and models), and they will be able to build me a custom-made driveshaft to connect my GM transmission to my Ford rear axle.

The other method calls for installing the old transmission U-joint yoke in the transmission to a point where the shiny wear pattern on the yoke just disappears into the oil seal. This is the normal ride position of the yoke. Then a measurement is taken from the center of one of the U-joint caps on the transmission yoke to the center of one of the U-joint caps on the rear axle. That's the length of the new driveshaft.

BACK AT THE ENGINE BRACKETS

When this car first came into the shop, the engine was already mounted to the frame. The mounting brackets were generic bolt-on aftermarket items, but they were solidly constructed, and I knew they could be easily cut and trimmed to adapt them to welded-into-place units.

For added strength, I wanted the brackets installed at a slight angle, about 20 degrees, as shown in photo

8. Had I cut the brackets so that they would sit level after installation, the weight of the engine would have placed undue stress on the welds, and eventual failure of the welds could have resulted. However, installing the brackets at an upward angle allows the weight of the engine to press outward on the brackets, thereby eliminating all stress on the welds. These brackets will be there until they push a hole through the cross member, which is very unlikely to occur.

Then there is the subject of motor mount bolts. These mounts are stock GM mounts, and they use three $\frac{5}{16}$ x 1-inch bolts to attach each mount to the engine and one $\frac{3}{8}$ x 4-inch bolt to connect the mount to the mounting bracket. All of these bolts must be grade 8 or stronger, particularly the 4-inch bolt, as it will be subject to sheer stresses. The garden variety home improvement center bolt won't do here.

SOME UNFINISHED FRAME TASKS

That leaves three things unfinished on this frame before the body can be installed. The first is constructing a new transmission mounting bracket. This proved to be a very easy task, as all that was needed was to shorten a 1994 Mustang transmission mounting bracket I had stashed at the shop and bolt it to the bottom side of the X-member. It is visible in photo 2.

The second task consists of building up the front suspension, as shown in photo 9. At a future date, I'll be routing the steering shaft, so that means the rack and pinion setup must already be mounted. I'll also want to mount the front fenders and fender skirts later, so I need to be sure no clearance problems exist around the control arms and steering linkages. It is far better to find clearance problems now, before the paint goes on, than later when I have to start hacking and welding on my fresh paint job.

The third issue concerns the emergency brake cables. I have them routed to a point just behind the transmission but no way to connect the cables to a brake handle. Notice in photo 10 that I mounted a rotating 1-inch steel tube underneath the rear arms of the X-member. Also notice the 1-inch-tall, 4-inch-long steel plate welded to the tube between the arms of the X-member. This plate serves as the mounting point for the brake cables. To keep the brake cables in place,

they are slipped into notches at each end of this plate and secured with an additional bolt-on top plate (photo 11). The top plate is removable should one or both of the brake cables ever need replacing.

In photo 12, you can see the elongated pull handle welded to the end of the tube. This will serve as the

PHOTO 8: A little cutting and trimming, and the bolt-on engine mounting brackets were converted to weld-on units.

PHOTO 9: At a later date, I'll be hanging front sheet metal around this suspension. It is better to find clearance problems now, before the paint goes on.

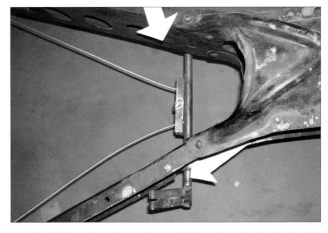

PHOTO 10: When the lever is rotated, or pulled forward, tension is placed on the cables, activating the rear brakes. Simple, but very effective.

PHOTO 11: The brake cables slip into notches cut in the bracket and are held secure by adding a plate on top of the bracket. The bolt allows easy removal of the plate should the cables ever need replacing.

PHOTO 12: Lengthening this pull handle will allow me to add an even longer adjustment bolt to ensure that the emergency brakes will activate with very little effort.

mounting point for a cable leading up to the brake handle inside the car. When the brake handle is pulled, the tube will rotate and apply tension to the brake cables attached to the center plate on the tube, thereby activating the rear brakes. Very effective.

Now throw into the mix the ability of the shock to resist side-to-side roll—that is, how much the vehicle leans as it moves into a deep curve—and suddenly the lowly shock has become something of a very important item to be considered when setting up a new suspension.

NOTES

CHAPTER 5

SHOCKS, SPRINGS, AND METAL LINES

Yesterday, the coil-over shocks for the rear axle arrived at the shop (photo 1). Now all I have to do is figure out where and how to mount them. In theory, a shock absorber's purpose in life is to resist, not prevent, the up-and-down movement of the suspension. But toss in the added feature of a coil-over spring, and you end up with an instrument that not only resists movement but also does the actual supporting of the suspension.

WHERE THE ACTION IS

Let's start with where and how to mount the coil-over shocks. The closer to the wheel the shock is mounted, the better it will perform. How so? If you hold the center of a broom handle with one hand and have someone pull down on one end, it is obvious all of the movement is happening at the ends of the handle, not in the center where you are holding it. The same thing occurs with a rear axle. The center of the axle doesn't move much when you run over a bump. All of the up and down movement is occurring out at the wheels. That is where the shocks need to be, out near the wheels and right in the middle of all of the action.

Next is the vertical placement of the shocks. The more vertically the shocks are mounted, the greater their dampening effect on the movement of the axle. Here are a couple of examples. If a shock is mounted 10 degrees from vertical, the shock will lose only 2 percent of its dampening ability. But if the shock is mounted 45 degrees from vertical, the loss of its dampening ability escalates to a whooping 40 percent!

So the bottom line here is that I need to look for mounting points as close to the wheels as possible without risk of the tires touching the shocks, and I need to mount the shocks as close to vertical as possible. So that's it?

Not quite. Rear coil-over shocks are available in a variety of load ratings and are known for their limited piston travel. As for load rating, spring manufacturers use a long mathematical formula based on vehicle weight, applied loads, the number of spring coils, wire diameters, and other factors to determine the load rating of a spring. This

PHOTO 1: These 250-lb-rated coil-over shocks will support the rear of the '46.

is important, as the spring must absorb only some of the load when in a static position. You don't want the weight of the vehicle to fully compress the shock while the vehicle is sitting still. The spring must be able to compress and expand according to the load placed on it.

So how do you determine what spring rating is correct for a particular vehicle? Fortunately, the major coil-over shock retailers have the formula already plugged into their computers, and all you have to do is provide the pertinent vehicle information such as year and model and overall weight in order to get the correct load springs. The '46 needs 250-lb springs for the rear shocks. The good news is that if I don't like the ride provided by the 250-lb springs, I can easily replace them with either softer or stiffer springs.

What does it mean to have springs rated at 250 lbs? It means that 250 lbs of downward force is required to compress the spring 1 inch.

MOUNTING THE SHOCKS

Now let's talk about shock travel. In this case, the piston travel from top to bottom is 7 inches. That means that when the suspension is setting at a static position, or normal ride height, I want the shock piston to be located at roughly the center point of its travel. Doing so will give me 3½ inches of shock travel both up and down.

Finding that perfect mounting point isn't so difficult with the Ford 8.8 rear axle. The swing arm mounting system allows me to place the axle at almost any height I desire, which I did at the beginning of this project. The factory shock mount locations found on the bottom of the axle just inboard of the wheels gives me the perfect place to mount the shocks. The only difficult part will be fabricating new brackets where the shocks extend up and mount to the frame.

PHOTO 2: An overall view of how the shocks are mounted. Notice the upper shock mounting bracket pieces welded to the underside of the frame rail. Also notice the axle stop (arrows), there to prevent the shocks from bottoming out and being damaged.

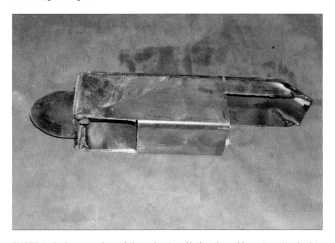

PHOTO 3: A close-up view of the axle stop. Notice the rubber stop attached to the bottom of the bracket.

Working on the left side, I start by mounting the shock to the axle assembly. By the way, I've removed the coil-over spring to make installation a little easier. Next, I extend the shock piston 3½ inches and look for a good mounting location for the upper mount. Since the shock is almost vertical when positioned directly under the frame rail, this makes the ideal mounting location; all I need to do is measure down from the bottom of the rail to the center of the upper shock mount to determine the length of my new brackets. Photo 2 shows how this was done.

Using a saber saw with a metal cutting blade, I cut four 1½ x 3-inch brackets from the ⅛-inch-thick plate steel purchased earlier, clamp the pieces together, and drill a ⅜-inch hole through all four brackets at once. This ensures the uniformity of the shock mounting holes. Next, I bolt two of the brackets to the shock, one on either side, using a grade 8, ⅜ x 2-inch bolt, position the brackets under the frame rail, and tack weld both pieces into place on the frame.

I repeat this exercise on the right side of the car, and when done I use a floor jack to move the rear axle up and down to be sure the shocks operate smoothly. All I'm looking for here is any indication the shocks might interfere with the movement of the axle. When satisfied all is well, I remove the shocks and finish welding the brackets to the frame.

ADDING AXLE STOPS

Considering that the operation of a typical shock absorber is to move up and down, I now need to be concerned with how much movement the shocks are subjected to. It isn't a great deal of concern for the shocks to fully extend as they would do if the body of the car were lifted straight up. What is of concern is the compression of the shocks. I don't want these coil-over shocks to ever completely bottom out, or fully compress. It could result in damage to the shocks. To prevent total compression of the shocks, I need to add axle stops to the suspension.

These are nothing more than brackets hanging down from the frame rails with rubber stops on the end designed to stop the upward travel of the rear axle before the shock absorbers become fully compressed (photo 3).

The brackets are simple enough. They are made from 2 x 2-inch square steel tubing with a rubber stop bolted to one end. The rubber stops come from a 1968 Mustang front lower control arm and are there to cushion the blow of the axle hitting the stop.

So the question is, how long do the stop brackets need to be? Since I don't want the shock absorbers to fully compress under any condition, I install the shocks back on the car and jack up the rear axle housing until approximately 1 inch of shock piston is visible at the top of the shocks. Next, I measure from the bottom of the frame rail to the top of the axle housing, in this case 4 inches. Subtract ½ inch to give the rubber stop room to compress, and now I know I need two brackets 3½ inches long. I construct the brackets, weld them into place, and verify the results by again jacking up the axle using the floor jack.

At this point, I could install the coil-over springs on the shocks, but without the full weight of the car on the suspension, all this would do is render my frame somewhat unstable. I'll leave the springs off for now and move on to the next item on the check list, the fuel tank.

RELOCATING THE GAS CAP

The original fuel tank had a side inlet with the fuel inlet door mounted on the left rear fender. My goal is to smooth out the exterior of this car, so I don't want an unsightly fuel door hanging off the left rear fender. I'll eventually make that door go away, but in the meantime I have to find a new place to mount a gas cap.

It may be that I've just completed the restoration of a Mustang, but for some strange reason I can easily see a Mustang fuel tank filling my needs. The Mustang tank comes with its own mounting flanges, would fit perfectly between the frame rails of this car, and has a rear fuel inlet. It is the rear fuel inlet part that really excites me. If I do this right, I can hide the inlet inside the trunk. Of course, there will be some issues with ensuring that the inlet is sealed off from the trunk compartment, but that's a matter to work on once I'm ready to install a new trunk floor pan. Right now I need to figure out how to mount the tank.

The important thing to remember here is to keep the tank level. Since the frame has already been leveled, all I need to do is support the tank in position, place a level on top of it, and fabricate new mounting brackets around it.

As you can see in photo 4, this installation proved to be very easy. I used the rear frame cross member to support the rear of the tank and built a new cross brace from 1-inch square tubing to support the front of the tank. The major things going on here include centering the gas tank between the frame rails to ensure that the fuel inlet will be centered in the car, fabricating the side mount brackets from a ⅛-inch steel plate (photo 5) and welding them to the cross bar used to support the front of the tank, and the use of the ever-present level to ensure that this tank remains level during installation.

Something else to be aware of is that this is a used tank and may still have gasoline fumes lingering inside of it. The first thing I did after removing the tank from storage was to send it out for cleaning. No way am I going to do fabrication work with an old tank filled with gasoline fumes.

PHOTO 4: Plenty of pointer arrows here. Notice the fuel inlet at the rear of the tank, the level used to ensure that the tank is level, and the brackets and support bar used to support the front of the tank.

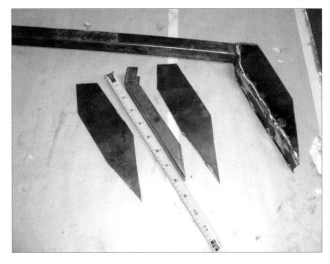

PHOTO 5: These are the side mount bracket pieces used to support the front of the fuel tank. Made from ⅛-inch plate steel, they are very sturdy.

BRAKE AND FUEL LINES

This discussion has to start with material selection. The choices are between mild steel and stainless steel. Mild steel may actually be the best choice when it comes to ease of installation. Mild steel can be easily bent into the correct shapes and can be hand molded to work it in and around all those obstacles between the front and the rear of the car. If mild steel has a drawback, it is that I've never seen a mild steel line that didn't need to be painted before installation.

Mild steel brake and fuel lines can be purchased in premade lengths or in bulk rolls. The shorter, premade pieces are usually the best option for car building, as the required double flares needed to seal the ends of the brake lines have already been made.

Stainless steel may look great when polished to a high luster, but your wallet will need to be a little thicker to afford this material, as stainless steel typically costs 50 to 100 percent more than mild steel. Until recently, stainless steel lines were sold in unflared straight lengths, which meant special equipment was needed to add the double flare to the ends of the lines. These days, premade, preflared lengths of stainless steel lines are available through the hot-rodding industry, and all you have to do is bend them to fit.

Whether you are constructing brake lines or fuel lines, I recommend using only two sizes of tubing, ³⁄₁₆ inch for the brake lines, which is pretty much the industry standard, and ⅜ inch for the fuel lines, large enough to flow fuel for either a carburetor or a fuel injection system. I also recommend purchasing premade lengths and joining the lengths together using brass unions. This eliminates the need to produce those mandatory double flares on the brake lines and makes installation much easier.

SPEAKING OF INSTALLATION . . .

Whether installing brake or fuel lines, the lines have to be bent. The trick is knowing where and how to bend each line. To start with, you must have a good tubing bender. Try

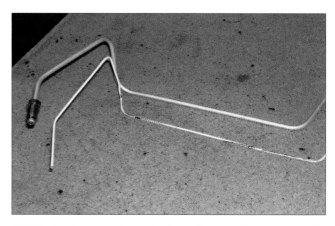

PHOTO 6: Coat hangers make great patterns. Here a coat hanger was used to pattern the front brake lines.

the Eastwood Triple Head Tubing Bender #49106, as it will accommodate both the ³⁄₁₆- and the ⅛-inch diameter tubes.

When bending the tubing, always work from one end to the other. Never start in the middle and work outward. Tubing stretches as it is drawn over the bender. If starting in the middle, the result will be that you will have too much tubing when you reach the end point.

Finally, how in the world do you get the length right when making a bend? Check out the illustrations. Figure 1 is the objective. Using the illustration, I make the first bend by measuring from the end of the tube to the tip of the tubing bender roller (figure 2). To make the next bend, I measure from the top center of the tubing bender roller to the center of the tube just past the bend, as shown in figure 3. Nothing to it.

To secure the new lines to the frame, I use stainless steel tubing clips (photo 7). These clips are perpetually available on eBay, or check your local hot rod parts dealer. Purchase the correct-size clips for the line being clamped, and space the clips every 3 to 4 feet along the frame and anywhere else the lines might vibrate or be subjected to chaffing.

To secure the clips to the frame, I use $\frac{3}{16}$ x $\frac{1}{2}$-inch stainless steel sheet metal screws. I also take the time to ensure that both the rear brake line and the fuel line are as protected as possible. That means routing the lines inside the frame rail where possible.

At this point, I'm not going to delve into routing the lines to the brake master cylinder or be concerned about adding a proportioning valve. What's a proportioning valve, and why don't I need one? A proportioning valve controls the rate of pressure buildup to the rear brakes. That means adding a proportioning valve would allow the rear brakes to apply a little slower than the front brakes, thus reducing the chances of the rear brakes locking up during braking. This car has four-wheel disc brakes, and normally that means the rear brakes don't tend to lock up during braking. Should locking up become a problem during the test run phase of this build, I can always add an adjustable proportioning valve between the master cylinder and the rear brakes to reduce the line pressure and the chances of the rear brakes locking up.

If your setup calls for disc brakes up front and drum brakes at the rear, then a proportioning valve will be necessary to prevent the rear drum brakes from locking up. I suggest purchasing an adjustable valve and following the instructions that come with the unit for proper operation.

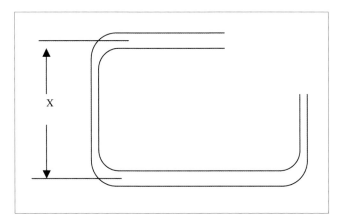

FIGURE 1

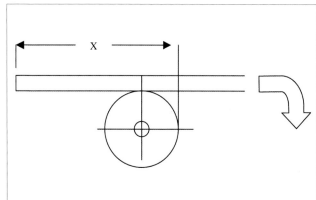

FIGURE 2

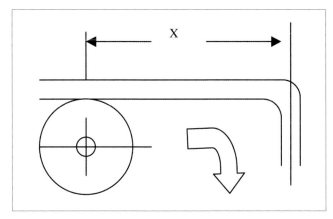

FIGURE 3

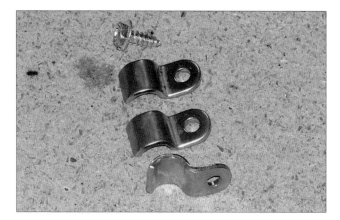

PHOTO 7: Stainless steel line fasteners should be spaced about every 3 feet.

NOTES

NOTES

CHAPTER 6

FLOOR PAN
INSTALLATION

One of the first things I did to help get this project off to a good start was to remove the body from the car and send it out for media blasting. What medium did I use to remove the old paint? Coal slag. Something new? To me it is. But as I understand it, this medium has been in use in other places for several years now. The coarse texture of coal slag makes it ideal for removing deep surface rust, thick paint, and aging plastic body fillers without harming the metal. That's exactly what this car needed. After having sat in a field for many years, what little paint that remained on the body was rock hard, and the areas where the old paint had eroded away were now covered in heavy surface rust. To add insult to injury, the entire body was speckled with spots of very thick, very aged plastic body filler.

MEDIA BLASTING AND RUST TREATING

As I thought about how to remove all of the above-mentioned problems, I also took into consideration the age and thickness of the metal making up this car. This was not a '60s muscle car made of thin metal, nor did it have any flat panels to speak of that might be warped or damaged by the media-blasting process. This was a big, round "boat" made of heavy steel, so it didn't seem likely that anything done to the car in the way of media blasting would cause any additional damage. Looking back now, I can see I made a good decision. The body came out nice and clean, and now I can move forward.

Of course, once the metal is blasted down to its bare shine, it will need some protection to keep sur-

face rust at bay while I bang out the dents and weld up the holes. For that, I turned to the Eastwood Company and opted to coat the inside of the car with its rust converter product.

Eastwood's rust converter is a two-part product, Rust Converter Part A #12556 and Rust Converter Part B #12558, developed specifically to kill existing rust by converting it to an extremely hard primer substrate. The media blasting process removed all of the visible rust, but I knew places existed inside this car where access with the media blaster was limited. It was this hidden rust that concerned me, so as soon as I had the cleaned body back in my possession, I used the Eastwood applicator gun #16003A and gave every square inch of the interior of the body a good heavy coat of Rust Converter.

Not to be placated by the fact that I had just rust treated the inside of this car with one of the best products out there, I followed that application by applying two coats of semigloss black Eastwood Rust Encapsulator #16065ZP to the outside of the body using the Binks M1-G HVLP. I've been to car shows and found cars that were in a "finished" state that didn't look much different. But that's another subject altogether.

> **TIP**
>
> *Be sure the person doing the actual media blasting knows to never touch the cleaned metal with his bare hands. The oils from your skin can contaminate the metal and prevent any coating applied over it from sticking properly.*

Why didn't I just pick one rust-inhibiting product and apply it everywhere? Eastwood's Rust Converter goes on very thick, and I liked the idea of having this heavy coating inside the car. Rust Encapsulator goes on a lot thinner, and since I'll eventually be covering the exterior of the car with epoxy, plastic body filler, and paint, I wanted something I could easily sand and paint over.

REMOVING THE OLD FLOOR PANS

Next on my punch list of things to do to this body is to remove the old floor pans. Yes, I know I just cleaned and rust treated everything, but once they were cleaned and treated, I decided the floor pans were in far worse condition than I had previously thought. I could have patched here and patched there, but considering how quick and easy the floor pans could be cut out of this car and replaced with new metal, trying to save the old pans just didn't make sense.

I know what you are thinking: this idiot just took all of the structural rigidity out of this car without adding any bracing. Well, I'm crazy, but I'm not that crazy. As you can see in photo 1, I built a square cage inside the car using 1-inch square steel tubing back before I sent the body out for media blasting. I added the cage to make lifting and moving the body a little easier. Fork lift operators seem to function better when you can point to an exact place where they can safely lift whatever needs lifting. This cage serves that purpose and will stay in place until the body is back on the frame, the floor pans have been replaced, and the top has been chopped.

A little time spent with an air chisel and die grinder makes short work of the old floor pan, and I'm ready to mount the body back on the frame. Don't forget the safety equipment, eye protection, ear protection, and heavy leather gloves when grinding and cutting metal.

To be sure the body sits on the frame at the correct height, I purchased a new rubber body mount kit from Steele Rubber Products. Installing new rubber body mounts ensures that the body sits on the frame correctly, so that when I fabricate the new floor pans, I won't end up with any problem areas where the body is touching the frame.

MAKING A FLOOR PAN TEMPLATE

A trip to the local hobby store netted me several 2 x 4-foot sheets of heavy construction paper ideal for template making. Guys in the upholstery business refer to this paper as chipboard and use tons of it to make templates for door panels, headliners, and a whole host of other interior pieces.

Since the floor pan area of the '46 is now little more than a huge void of metal, I also made a trip to the local metal mart, where I procured two 4 x 8-foot sheets of 16-gauge steel, plus four 8-foot lengths of $\frac{1}{4}$ x 1-inch bar stock. The sheet steel will become my new floor pan, and the bar stock will be used as reinforcing bars to give the floor pan added strength. I'll also use the bar stock to form the framework for the driveshaft tunnel, which can be seen in photo 2.

To position the reinforcing bars inside the car, I laid one across the floor at the front of the door opening and

PHOTO 1: Knowing the body would need to be stiffened prior to removing the floor pans and chopping the top, I added this square steel tubing framework.

PHOTO 2: The right side of the floor pan. Notice the bar stock used to help support the floor pan and form a framework for the squared driveshaft tunnel.

the other across the floor at the rear of the door opening. Each bar is centered inside the car, then cut and welded to form the hat shape needed for the driveshaft tunnel. Both pieces are then welded to the inboard side of the rocker panels, taking care that each bar is flush with the top of the rocker panel. This method allows me to lay the new floor pans on top of the rocker panels, where they can be easily welded into place.

To make cutting and sizing the floor pan templates a little easier, I start by placing a single sheet of construction paper inside the car and rough cutting the sheet to fit. Next, I carefully trim the sheet down to the exact size needed to simulate a portion of the new floor. As each piece of construction paper is cut and laid into place, I mark it as to location, such as left front, left rear, then use masking tape to secure the template to the rocker panel and keep the piece from shifting or moving. As my new template begins to grow in size, I add more tape around the edges of the construction paper so that each piece is securely joined to the next piece until I have formed a single template of the entire floor pan (photo 3). With that done, the huge template can be removed from the car.

This is my new floor pan template (photo 4). But the plan doesn't call for constructing a single-piece floor pan to try to shoehorn back into the car. That would be extremely difficult, if not impossible. To keep life simple, I cut the template into six separate sections: two pieces for the front, two pieces for the rear, and two pieces for the driveshaft tunnel.

Once cut apart, the template pieces are positioned on the 16-gauge steel sheet, and the new floor pans are marked for cutting. For marking, I prefer using a metal scribe, and once marked I go back and outline the cut with ¾-inch-wide masking tape.

To do the actual cutting, I prefer to use pneumatic metal cutting shears—try the Eastwood #28118—or a good die grinder—try the Eastwood 3" Composite Body Cut-Off Tool #28024, with a 3-inch cutoff wheel attached. If neither tool is collecting dust in your tool box, opt for a good jigsaw with a metal cutting blade or a very good pair of hand-operated metal cutting shears. But no matter which tool you finally use, don't forget a pair of leather gloves, and eye and ear protection.

As for installing the new floor pans, I start with the passenger's side front piece, as this piece will need to be bent to roughly a 40-degree angle, where the toe kick portion of the pan slopes up to meet the firewall. A look at photo 5 shows this bend. Once the new floor pan piece has been bent, it is laid in the car and checked for fit. All I'm looking for here is to be sure the bend is in the correct place and the pan lays flush with the rocker panel and firewall. Once I know the pan fits, I remove it from the car and drill it for spot welding.

TIP

Cut the new floor pans to lay flat in the car, and cut the new driveshaft tunnel so that it can be bent on a metal brake—try the Eastwood 36" Sheet Metal Brake #28025 unit—and shape the tunnel like a hat, with a 1-inch-wide brim. The 1-inch-wide brim, or flange, will allow the new tunnel to sit on top of the new floor pan. The flanges, one on either side of the new tunnel, can be drilled for spot welding; space each 5/16-inch hole 2 inches apart, and weld directly to the floor pan.

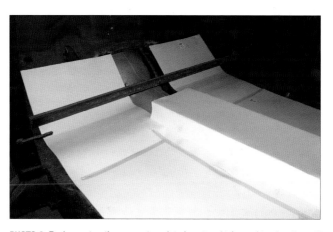

PHOTO 3: Each construction paper template is cut and trimmed to size, then all are taped together to form the new floor pan and tunnel.

PHOTO 4: The completed template for the new floor pan.

PHOTO 5: The right front floor pan and front section of the driveshaft tunnel. Notice the angled portion of the floor pan, referred to as the toe kick. This area of the floor pan angles up to meet the firewall.

PHOTO 7: Notice the flanges at the rear of the old driveshaft tunnel. These were added to serve as a mounting platform for the new rear tunnel piece. (You can ignore the arrows pointing out the bracing.)

The spot weld holes are drilled to 5/16 inch and spaced 2 inches apart along the rocker panel edge and across the top where the panel meets the firewall. After that, the piece is laid back in the car and secured into place using blind holders. What's a blind holder? Check out photo 6. This is a blind holder tool along with two blind holders. You might call these temporary rivets, as the tool allows the holder to be inserted in a 1/8-inch hole, then removed as needed. Yes, Eastwood has a kit for that, #19074. Barring the use of blind holders, you can use 1/2-inch #8 sheet metal screws to secure the pan for welding.

Once this pan is in place, the right rear pan goes in, followed by the two pans making up the driver's side of the floor pan. The left front pan will need the same 40-degree bend I gave the right front pan, and once that is done it is just a matter of securing the pans with more blind holders before moving on to the driveshaft tunnel.

The new driveshaft tunnel doesn't present much more of an installation problem than did the floor pans with the exception of the forwardmost 12 inches and the rear attachment point. At the rear, I formed the welding flanges visible in photo 7 from the L-shaped metal brackets to serve as an attachment point for the tunnel. You can ignore the arrows in the photo unless you are interested in where I attached the bracing used to help stabilize the body while cutting out the floor pans.

The front portion of the tunnel cannot be fabricated until the new floor pans and the driveshaft tunnel pieces are in place. To make this piece, I once again form a paper template, transfer that to metal, bend and shape the piece, then weld it into place (photo 8).

To weld all of these pieces, I generally do a single weld, move at least 12 inches away, and make another

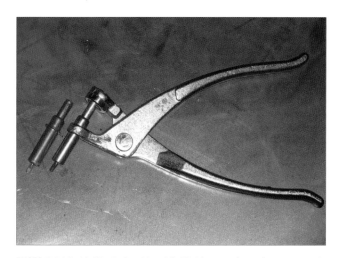

PHOTO 6: A blind holder tool and two blind holders, used anywhere two panels are joined. After welding, the holders can be removed and used elsewhere.

PHOTO 8: This front portion of the driveshaft tunnel could not be fabricated until the floor pans and driveshaft tunnel pieces had been installed.

weld. I continue this pattern until all of the spot weld holes are welded solid, all of the screws or blind holders are removed, and all of the resulting attachment holes are welded shut. This method reduces the chances of heat warping the pans by disbursing the heat evenly across the panels.

MY TRUNK WENT WHERE?

The trunk floor pan has to be approached from a different angle. Back here, my objective is to level the floor and in so doing give me a way to install a hidden fuel inlet compartment inside the trunk compartment.

The forward section of the trunk originally had a stepped area to bring the floor pan up and over the rear axle. From there, it gently sloped downward all the way back to the rear body panel. This is a huge, roomy trunk, and I knew it had ample space to allow me to raise the rear portion of the floor enough to accommodate fabricating a fuel inlet compartment at the rear of the trunk.

I start by laying a 6-foot carpenter's level lengthwise in the trunk, with one end on the stepped portion of the old floor and the other end extended toward the rear of the trunk. I level the level, then measure the space from the old floor pan up to the bottom of the carpenter's level at the rear of the compartment. That measurement is roughly 6 inches. Next, I cut out the old trunk floor pan but leave the original compartment area that is visible in photo 9. The two round holes visible in this panel are the rear body-to-frame mounting holes, thus the reason for leaving this panel intact. Using my 6-inch measurement, I fabricate the new rear floor pan support panel also seen in photo 9.

Putting my template maker's hat back on, I divide the trunk into a front half and a rear half and make templates of both sections. Both pieces are about as basic as floor pans can be in that the rear half is a simple flat panel and the front half is a simple flat panel with the forwardmost 8 inches bent down at a 45-degree angle to serve as a step to lift the pan up and over the rear axle. This angled portion of the pan is visible in photo 7.

To give the new floor pan added support, I construct the channeled cross member seen in photo 10 and place it so that both pieces of the new floor can be welded to it. That makes the floor strong enough to hold all the luggage I could hope to stuff inside here, but it won't stop the new pans from vibrating or popping any time a load

is placed on them. To further stiffen the pans, I add the beads shown in photo 11 using the Eastwood #28187 Bead Roller Kit. The beads are placed on the diagonal three to a side and act to really solidify my new floor.

PHOTO 9: To gain a level trunk floor pan, I had to raise the rear of the pan several inches. This worked out great in that it gave me a place to install a hidden fuel filler inlet.

PHOTO 10: The cross member seen here helps support the new trunk floor pan.

PHOTO 11: Here you can see how the beads were rolled into the floor pan to give the pan additional strength.

In photo 11, notice how clean this new trunk compartment has become. Notice also the large flat door at the rear of the compartment and the square hole just forward of the door. This hole will allow me access to the fuel tank filler tube should I ever need to remove the fuel tank from the car. Later, when I know I won't need access to the fuel tank, I'll cap this hole with a screwed-down plate.

The large door will serve as access to the fuel inlet. Made of 16-gauge steel, it is strong enough to support almost anything a person can toss into the trunk. It is hinged to the floor pan using a full-length piano-type hinge that is temporarily bolted in place. Once all of the fabrication work has been completed, I'll toss the bolts in favor of buck-type aluminum rivets. These are not pop rivets; this type of rivet must be installed using an air hammer with a rivet driver and a handheld dolly.

Inside this compartment, I fabricate a box for the fuel inlet tube (photo 12). At a later date, I'll add a rear license plate pocket back here, and just to be sure this area is secure and completely isolated from the trunk compartment, I'll also add a lock to the compartment door.

PHOTO 12: This is the fuel inlet compartment, which is isolated from the trunk compartment by the large door. Any gasoline fumes that are created when fueling the car will be vented to the outside via drainage holes in the bottom of the compartment.

NOTES

_____

_____

_____

_____

_____

_____

_____

_____

_____

NOTES

CHAPTER 7

INSTALLING
"SUICIDE" DOORS

really enjoyed not having doors on this car as I went about rust treating the body and replacing the floor pans. But the time has come to make crawling in and out of this car a little more difficult by hanging the doors. The time has also come to decide how these doors will hang. Do I put them back the way they were supposed to be installed, with the hinges mounted at the front, or do I make a major change and reverse the hinges so that the doors open in the opposite direction, sometimes referred to as suicide doors?

In the end, I opt to reverse the doors and go with the suicide setup. This was a cool way to build a hot rod some years ago, and since I can't seem to shake my old-school mentality, making the switch just seems to come naturally. Of course, such a drastic change means purchasing new hinges designed for the reverse-swing doors. While I'm in the shopping mode, I'll also purchase new bear claw–type latches, complete with remote-controlled electric actuators. The new latches will ensure that these doors stay securely closed, and the electric actuators will let me shave off the outside door handles and give this car a very sleek look.

HIDING THAT LOWER HINGE

If you have ever taken a close look at a '46 Ford, you may have noticed the lower door hinges are exposed. Why would these hinges be exposed? Hinges work best when they are aligned vertically. The body of this car is shaped like an egg, with the doors tapering inboard at the bottom. To keep the upper and lower hinges vertically aligned, the lower hinge pivot point has to be placed outboard of the door frame by about 1½ inches.

Now check out photo 1 for the new goodies I'll use to convert the doors to suicide opening. These new hinges are constructed so that even though I'll be reversing the swing of the doors, the lower hinges will not be exposed. How did they do that? I'll start by explaining the construction of the old hinges.

These old hinges are not much different from the hinges on a bathroom door. They are basically flat plates of steel with the hinge pivot points located at the edge of the hinges. It is this pivot point on both the upper and lower hinges that must be in vertical alignment for the hinges to work properly.

The new hinges are constructed much differently. They use J-shaped swing arms that allow the hinge pivot points to be moved inboard about 1½ inches. With the pivot points moved inboard, the lower hinges can be relocated and basically hidden from view, in this case inside the quarter panels.

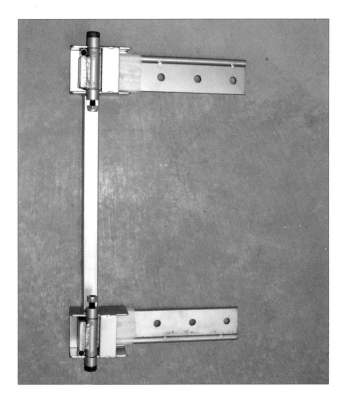

PHOTO 1: These hinges, commonly referred to as suicide hinges, are designed to convert the doors from a front hinge setup to a rear hinge setup.

PHOTO 2: Bear claw latches are available in kit form. You get everything you need to install this latch, from the latch assembly to the mounting plate to a new striker bolt.

PHOTO 3: The door frame has been cut open to receive the new hinge swing arm mounting plates. The plate steel is used for added reinforcement to strengthen the door frame.

Notice also in the photo that the new upper and lower hinges are connected via a square steel tube. This steel connector tube ensures that the hinges remain parallel to and in vertical alignment with each other during mounting; that in turn eliminates any fitting problems that can arise from misaligned hinges. Can misaligned hinges really cause me that much trouble? Yes, they can. For example, misaligned hinges can throw a door out of balance when it is opened. The door will seem to have a will of its own and literally throw itself open, maybe pulling you right out of the car in the doing. OK, a good seat belt can deal with that, but it can't deal with the problem of the door rubbing the quarter panel every time it is opened or closed. Now that's a hinge misalignment problem worth correcting, which is exactly why the hinge alignment bar is there.

Once the new hinges are installed and the doors open and close the way they should, I need to be sure the doors stay securely shut when closed. To take care of that detail, I opt to scrap the old door latches in favor of a set of modern bear claw–type latches.

Available in kit form (photo 2), this style of latch comes with everything needed to make the latch conversion, including a new latch assembly, latch-mounting plate, and the correct-size striker bolt. Striker bolts come in different sizes? Yes, they do. To be sure the bolt fits the latch, never purchase a latch that doesn't come with a striker bolt. But I'm getting ahead of myself talking about the latches. Right now I need to concentrate on hinging these doors.

DOORS THAT REALLY SWING

To convert these doors to suicide opening, I want the new hinges positioned so that they will carry the bulk of the weight of the door yet still be mounted in such a way as to not interfere with the operation of the door glass.

The doors on the '46 are very shallow, less than 4 inches thick, and as mentioned previously have a very definite curve to them. That doesn't leave a lot of room to recess the new hinge swing arm mounting plates into the doors, which you can see happening in photo 3, and still provide clearance for the door glass when it is rolled up or down.

Why recess the swing arm mounting plates, and what am I going to do with the huge steel plate visible in photo 3? Again, this car has very shallow doors, and one of the features of this type of door is a large, flat door trim panel. To get the new trim panel to lay flat on the door, the swing arm mounting plates must be recessed into the framework of the door.

The oversized steel plate is made from 16-gauge sheet metal and will eventually be welded to both swing arm mounting plates and to the inside face of the door. It is put there to add extra strength to the door frame where I hacked it apart to accept the mounting plates.

On the quarter panel side, I want the hinge bodies mounted in a location where access to the hinge bolts won't present a problem. Since I'll be welding the hinge bodies to the door posts, I'll need access to these bolts later on in order to remove the hinge swing arms for painting.

So taking into consideration both the need to hack apart the door frame to install the swing arm mounting plates and the need to avoid the door glass once the mounting plates are installed, I settled on placing the upper hinge mounting point 6 inches down from the door glass opening, which automatically places the lower hinge 10 inches up from the bottom of the door. This places the upper swing arm mounting plate at the widest point of the door body, and that will ensure that I have just enough clearance for the door glass to slip past the mounting plate any time the glass is rolled up or down. The position of the lower hinge mounting plate won't present a problem, as the door glass does not roll down that far.

The door measurements are then transferred to the door posts on the quarter panels, where I cut square holes the same size as the hinge mounting boxes, roughly 2 x 2 inches. Notice in photo 4 that the hole for the lower hinge sits farther outboard on the quarter panel than does the upper hinge mounting hole. Again, the body of this car is very tapered. This offset is necessary to keep both hinges in vertical alignment.

ASSEMBLING THE PARTS

Working on each door, and having the openings for the new hinges cut into both the door and the door post, it is time to put all of the pieces together.

The one thing I can't afford is to end up with a door not fitting the car once the hinge installation is finished. To be sure that doesn't happen, I use a floor jack to lift and position the door on the car. Once the door is aligned in the door opening, I tack weld it into place using small metal taps at each corner of the door (photo 5). You might call this instant door alignment. What it does is ensure that the door is in the correct position on the car before the hinges are installed and any welding is done.

> **TIP**
>
> *To be sure the door has even gaps all around, use the Eastwood Panel Gap Gauge #31129.*

The next step is to install the new hinges and tack weld them into place. I start by inserting the hinge bodies through the square openings in the door post and letting the hinge swing arms extend through the openings and out into the slotted openings cut into the door frame.

After that, the hinge swing arm mounting plates are slid into place inside the door frame and bolted to the swing arms using the countersunk head bolts provided in the hinge kit.

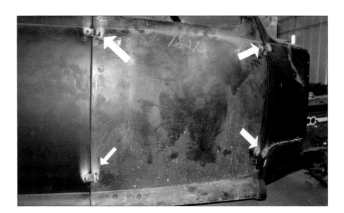

PHOTO 4: Square holes are cut in the quarter panel door post to accept the hinge boxes.

PHOTO 5: Instant door alignment. To ensure that the door fits once I weld the hinges in place, I first welded the door in place on the car.

PHOTO 6: This definitely looks crude, if not somewhat shade tree. But bear in mind that nothing seen here can be securely welded into place until I know both hinges are in perfect position. Once I know that, I'll make this all pretty.

Refer to photo 6 above. A lot is going on here, so let's start with the door. If it looks as if I've seriously compromised the integrity of the door by hacking it apart to accept the new swing arm mounts, you're right, I have. But at this point, that isn't a problem. I had to open up the framework of the door in order to insert the new mounting plates into the door, and this was the best way to gain that space without chopping the door completely apart. The 16-gauge plate steel shown earlier will help me regain that lost integrity once it is welded into place.

Also notice in the photo that I have installed all six of the bolts used to attach the hinge swing arms to the mounting plates. This ensures proper alignment between the mounting plates and the swing arms, so that when everything is welded into place and the door is removed from the car to complete the welding, it can be easily reinstalled without a lot of fuss trying to realign things.

Next, I tack weld the swing arm mounting plates to the door frame as well as tack weld the hinge mounting boxes to the door post. I know things look a little crude at this point, like mounting a chrome bumper on a Honda, but it will all work out.

Finally, notice the vertical hinge-support bar I added inside the quarter panel to help stabilize the hinge mounting boxes. This ¼ x 1-inch steel bar is tack welded to the floor pan, to both hinge mounting boxes, and to the quarter glass surround structure. The Vise-Grips are there in case I need to cut a tack weld and move one of the hinges.

At this point, I'm really not concerned with the absence of anything inside the quarter panel that is structurally sound enough to hold the hinges in place. I'll add additional reinforcement pieces to help stabilize the

hinges a little later, after I know my hinges are positioned where they need to be positioned and the door opens and closes without binding in the opening or rubbing the edge of the quarter panel.

CHECKING FOR SAG AND FIT

Something I am concerned about is making sure the door glass clears the upper swing arm mounting plate. This is strictly a visual inspection sort of thing, and once I'm sure the glass will not bind on the mounting plate, I can move on.

Moving on means using a die grinder with a 3-inch cutoff wheel attached to cut off the metal tabs previously welded to the outside of the door. I'm going to watch the door very closely as I cut the tabs. Any indication that the door is trying to sag or otherwise move out of alignment with the body raises a red flag. My only recourse at that point would be to once again position the door back on the car, weld the tabs back into place, and add more reinforcing or more welds to the hinges to solidify their positions.

Luckily, no such problems arose, and the door opened and closed just fine. Of course, there are things to look for listed under the "just in case" category. For example, both of the doors on the '46 are a very snug fit in the door openings. I want to be sure that when the doors are opened and closed neither one touches the door opening frames anywhere. If one of the doors did touch, I would need to cut at least one of the hinges loose and shift the door to gain the needed clearance.

> **TIP**
>
> *An area to closely scrutinize is the rear edges of the doors, where they move past the leading edge of the quarter panels. If either of the doors rub in this area, it would be a sign that the door was mounted too far inboard or too far back in the opening. Again, time to cut welds and shift a hinge.*

OPEN "SEZ ME"

Turning my attention to latching these doors, I start by determining where on the doors to place the latch assemblies. In this case, that point is 16 inches up from the bottom of the door, or roughly near the middle of the door. Why near the middle? Open any car door you prefer, and you will find the latch positioned at roughly the midway point between the door glass opening and the bottom of the door. This is the optimum point for securely holding a door in place and keeping it in good alignment with the car.

As you can see in photo 7, once this style of latch is closed and the clasps, or "claws," are wrapped around the striker bolt, it isn't going to come open accidentally. This is about as secure a latch as you are going to find anywhere.

The actual installation of this latch is pretty straightforward. All I need to do is cut a hole in the door frame for the new latch, fit the new latch mounting plate to the hole, weld in the mounting plate, and bolt on the latch. What could be easier? Well, a lot of things, like going to the dentist, or getting a tetanus shot. OK, I happen to like my dentist, and what could be more enjoyable than relaxing in a doctor's waiting room while he sharpens his needle?

But I digress. Notice the finished latch installation in photo 8. The latch is actually recessed into the frame of the door. Why the recess? With the door closed, the space separating the door from the door post is only ¼ inch. That's not much clearance when you consider I have three bolts protruding from the latch into that space and a striker bolt with a flat washer attached also taking up some of that space. Add to that the possibility that the striker bolt could actually penetrate too deeply into the latch and cause a binding issue, and it becomes quite apparent that a little more room is needed between the door post and the latch.

Photo 9 shows the fabrication step of cutting the door and fitting the latch mounting plate. The actual recess back from the framework of the door is ⅜ inch. The voids between the latch mounting plate and the door frame are filled with ⅜-inch-wide strips of 16-gauge steel and welded solid. Referring back to photo 8, you can see how clean this fabrication step makes the latch look.

Now take a look at photo 10. You can see I've already positioned and tack welded the striker plate to the door post. To reach this point, I closed the door with the new latch already mounted and marked the center of the latch on the door post using a permanent ink pen. Next, I laid the striker plate over the door post and aligned the striker bolt hole in the mounting plate over my mark. Then, I traced around

the striker plate to give me a pattern for cutting the opening in the door post.

The actual cuts are made using a die grinder with a metal-cutting 3-inch cutoff wheel attached. That brings me to the point seen in the photo. I tack welded the plate into place, screwed in the striker bolt, and

PHOTO 7: This style of latch has two steel "claws" that wrap around the striker bolt when closed. Once closed, this latch is almost impossible to break open. That's why you see this type of latch on many modern vehicles.

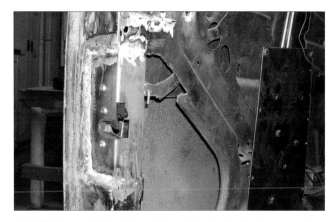

PHOTO 8: The completed latch installation. Notice that the latch is recessed into the door frame. This recess ensures that the latch will clear the striker bolt when the door is closed.

PHOTO 9: The door frame has been cut out and the latch mounting plate has been tack welded into place.

PHOTO 10: The latch striker plate has been recessed into the door frame and tack welded into place.

PHOTO 11: Here is the completed striker plate installation welded and ground smooth.

closed the door. This is the only way to be sure the two components align. If the door refused to shut or had a tendency to bind on the striker bolt, it would be time to cut welds and make a striker plate adjustment or two.

The good news is that the striker bolt hole in the striker plate is large enough to allow the striker bolt to be shifted up, down, in, or out as needed. Once I have the striker bolt adjusted and the latch working perfectly, I can finish welding the striker plate to the door post and grind the welds smooth.

As you can see in photo 11, the conversion is complete. You can also see one of the reasons I needed to recess the latch into the door frame. The washer on this striker bolt sticks out about ⅛ inch.

So how does the door look after all of the modifications? Photo 12 gives you a good look at the results of all my hacking and welding. This may be the strongest part of the entire car.

PHOTO 12: The driver's door, complete with new swing arm mounting plates and steel plate reinforcement.

NOTES

CHAPTER 8

CHOPPING
THE TOP

I once had the occasion to ask a guy how many inches had been removed from the chopped top on his car. He shrugged. He wasn't sure. He had simply cut until he thought the car looked about right and started welding. Hearing that gave me cold chills. That is not how I do things. I may occasionally shoot from the hip, but when I do I'm coming from the standpoint of having been there, done that several times already. The rest of the time I make a plan.

Speaking of standpoints, this isn't my first rodeo with a top chop, and it probably won't be my last. What this is, is a task that can be extremely difficult to complete if not well thought out and executed carefully and an absolute disaster if not done right.

SOME BAD EXAMPLES

Case in point: I once sat in a car with a roof that had been so drastically chopped all you could see from the driver's seat was the sun visor. Forget about seeing the traffic lights at an intersection or for that matter very much of the actual traffic surrounding you. The car might have been stunning to look at when parked, but it was nothing short of a wreck waiting to happen when out on the road.

Then there is the car that has been chopped so haphazardly that no attention to detail has been paid and the results are nothing short of comical. Last, there is the chop job that cost a bundle and was done extremely well but with so little removed from the roof that it left the occasional observer to wonder if the top had been chopped at all. That, my friends, was a huge waste of time and money.

What am I getting at with all this rambling about chopped tops? Tops are never chopped just for the sake of chopping a top. The act is done to enhance the looks of the car, not to make it a driving hazard, turn it into a comedy, or to leave you guessing.

START WITH A VIRTUAL CHOP

I find it very handy to have close acquaintances in the printing business. That allows me to shoot a few digital side shots of the car about to be chopped, deliver the shots to the print shop, and order up a few 12 x 16 blowups of the car, such as the one shown in photo 1. What is this shot for and what's with the masking tape over the door opening?

This picture is going to let me chop the top on this car without ever picking up a tool. The tape is there to provide me with reference points to help determine how much chop to give this top.

Here's how I did it. I laid down the first tape line using 1½-inch-wide masking tape. The goal here is to establish a straight line from which to work. The wide tape helps me do that. Next, I took ¾-inch wide-masking tape and spaced several strips ¾ of an inch apart along the side of the car above the 1½-inch-wide tape. That lets me use a few of the blowup side shots of the car as guinea pigs as I crop and cut each shot using the tape lines as reference points. I literally chop the top on this car without ever putting a saw to the metal. Yes, the print shop could have accomplished the same thing on the computer screen, but as I've mentioned before I'm old school, and being able to put scissors to the pictures suits me better. Besides, I can crop the pictures all I want, tack the finished product on the wall, and know basically what the top chop will look like when finished. I've found laptops don't work very well once you've nailed them to the wall.

For this car, I decided a chop of 3 inches looked best. How did I determine that? By cropping the photos and using the tape lines as reference points, as mentioned above, I cropped and lowered the top one tape line at a time until I got the top chop I was looking for. In this case, as you can see in photo 2, I removed the top two tape lines, thereby lowering the top by 3 inches. Not too much, but definitely enough to know the top has been chopped.

WHERE DO I START?

I don't start by hacking and chopping; I start with a cutting plan. For anyone who has ventured down this road before, it

PHOTO 1: Chopping a top always starts by finding a way to see the end result. Here I'm using a blowup shot of the car that can be cropped and cut to show the final result.

PHOTO 2: Here is the result of my picture cropping. This is what the car will look like once the top has been chopped.

is common knowledge that on most cars, when a portion of the windshield post is removed and the roof is lowered, the roof panel must slide forward to realign with the shortened windshield posts. Generally, that is accomplished by cutting the roof panel in half across the middle, sliding the front portion forward to meet the windshield posts, then fabricating a new roof section to fill the resultant gap.

That's a huge undertaking and extremely difficult to get right. Fortunately, that won't be necessary in this case. Look at the back glass visible in photo 3. To begin with, this is a very small opening. Taking 3 inches out of this opening to lower the roof panel would render it almost useless as a means of monitoring the traffic behind you. What I propose to do is remove the necessary 3 inches of metal from the windshield and door posts, then slice along the length of the sail panel area on each side of the car. This won't free the roof from the car because it will still be attached at the rear, but it will remove enough of the roof's structure to allow the entire roof panel to drop and slide forward. In effect, this will allow the back glass to fall forward and lie flatter. This method will not only result in accomplishing the top chop but will also add to the sleekness of the car by removing some of the bubble look.

The first step is to brace the body to make it rigid once the roof panel is cut loose. What happens if I don't add the bracing? Believe it or not, the body of this car, and that goes for just about every other car out there, is under a lot of stress from having been shaped from a lot of flat sheets of steel and all welded together. If I didn't add bracing to the inside of this body to hold everything rigid and in place once I cut the windshield posts apart, the body would pop apart like a can of biscuits left too long in the warm sunshine.

To brace this car, I use 1 x 1–inch square steel tubing and construct a box inside the car that is welded to the

PHOTO 3: The plan calls for leaving this small back glass opening intact by merely allowing the roof to fall forward.

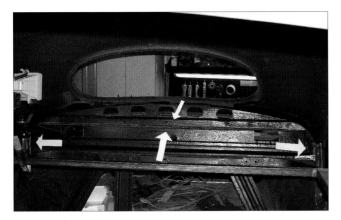

PHOTO 4: As far as package trays go, this isn't much of one. But I'll have to cut this one free of the car before the roof can be moved.

floor, the cowl, and the package tray area. You can actually see part of this bracing in photo 4. But please keep reading because that's not the reason I'm showing you photo 4.

Notice that in photo 4 you can see the rear package tray reinforcement panel extending across the back of the passenger compartment. This panel must be removed for the roof to drop down and slide forward. I'm going to remove it by cutting it free of the car where the arrows indicate. Once I have the roof moved forward and welded into place, I'll trim this panel down to size and weld it back in the car.

PLACING THE CUTS

The next step is to determine where the two windshield posts and the two center door posts will be cut. Photo 5 shows the cutting points on the left center door post. Notice that I placed the cutting points as near to the top of the post as possible. I'll get into the why of selecting these points for cutting a little later. Right now, I need to make my cuts. Notice also that I wrapped masking tape around the door post to mark the cutting points. The tape actually serves two purposes: first, it gives me a very visible line to follow when making my cuts; and second, the tape helps keep my cut lines straight. This is an important step, as the plan is to remove a section of post, then rejoin the cut ends. To effectively do that, both cuts must be square to each other. The tape ensures that will happen.

Photo 7 gives you an idea of how to go about cutting the top from the car. Notice that the posts have all been cut and the 3-inch section of each post has been removed, but the roof hasn't dropped. That's because I braced the top with an additional length of 1-inch square tubing to hold the roof up and prevent the top from sagging and binding with my saw. I used Vise-Grip pliers and clamped an additional length of tubing between the cage and the top of the windshield opening. You can also see in the photograph more of the cage I constructed inside the car to hold the body rigid.

PHOTO 5: I marked this door post for cutting by wrapping it with masking tape. The masking tape ensures that my cut lines will be square to each other.

PHOTO 6: The cutting tool of choice is a reciprocating saw with a metal cutting blade.

PHOTO 7: To prevent the roof from falling as the posts are being cut, I added more bracing to hold the roof up.

After cutting the necessary 3 inches out of each post, the next step is to cut slits along the length of both sail panels (photo 8). The slits start roughly 8 inches forward of the deck lid opening and extend forward all the way to a point roughly 8 inches forward of both center door posts. These slits serve one purpose: to free the roof panel from the quarter panels and allow it to move for-

ward. While we're here, make a mental note of the template you can see taped to the door window frame. I made a template of the entire door window frame, then cut the template down to size to simulate the chopped door. I'll talk about this template later, but for now it's back to the roof chop.

To pull the chopped top forward, I fastened a ratcheting cable puller to each side of the roof and extended both units down the frame (photo 9). All I have to do now is ratchet the cables and watch the roof move forward. The result of all this pulling can be seen in photo 10. The roof came forward quite easily, and because I took the time to ensure all of my cuts were made square to each other, the two pieces fit together nicely.

PHOTO 8: The roof panel can't slide forward until it is freed from the quarter panels. To free the roof panel, I cut slits along each sail panel.

PHOTO 9: Ratcheting cable pullers are used to pull the roof panel forward and down.

WELD THE OUTER AND INNER STRUCTURES

To secure the roof, I need to make a few welds at the windshield posts. But because the windshield posts are constructed in three layers, I'll need to cut an access hole in the outer layer of metal in order to reach the inner structure for welding. This is very important. Simply welding around the outer edges of the posts and not welding the inner structure will result in a very weak repair. Photo 11 shows how I opened the right windshield post for welding. At a later point in the top chop, I'll fold this flap back down and weld it solid. Why not do that now? Right now, I'm concerned with aligning all aspects of this chop. I'll leave this flap open until I know for sure I won't need to cut these welds loose and move the top.

Going back a few paragraphs, remember the template I made of the right door window frame (photo 8)? I'll use this template now to determine where to make my cuts on the door to bring the top of the door down to match my new

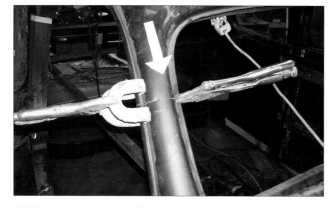

PHOTO 10: This is what I'm looking for: the roof pulled forward and down, and a perfect fit.

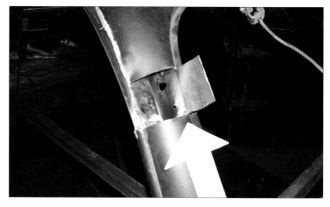

PHOTO 11: To weld the reinforcing metal inside the windshield post, I had to cut an access opening in the outer layer of metal.

roofline. Refer to photo 12. The arrows indicate where I'll make my cuts. Why make an extra cut at the top center of the frame? Once the top of the door window frame has been chopped and lowered, it will no longer have the correct length. I'll need to add metal in this area to provide that needed length. You can see evidence of this created space in photo 13, where a gap exists in the roofline above the door opening. I'll talk about that problem in a moment, but for now, back to the door.

Notice that my front and rear door window frame cut lines are below the cut lines made on the door post and windshield opening. This is an alignment issue and the very reason I made the cut on the center door post as high as possible. Remember I said earlier that I wanted to make my post cuts as close to the roof as possible? By offsetting all of my cuts, I am left with straight edges around the door opening from which I can align my cut edges. Believe me, this method makes life much easier when it comes to repositioning lopped off chunks of metal.

Now let's talk about photo 13. To start with, notice the gap in the roof panel above the door opening. This gap was created when I moved the upper door post section back to align it with the quarter glass opening. Notice also that I've already welded a small metal plate across the lower portion of the gap. This is necessary to help stabilize the door opening and ensure that it remains perfectly straight and true to the roof panel. Now notice the cut line above the repositioned upper door post section. This is the forward termination point for the slit I cut along the sail panel that allowed the roof to move forward.

Let's move to photo 14. You are still looking at the right door post. Notice that I've cut, moved, and welded two pieces of the upper quarter glass opening. Like the windshield and door openings, the quarter glass opening had to be narrowed to fit the new roofline. Cutting the two pieces out of the opening and repositioning them was necessary to maintain the natural curve of the opening.

Now notice the void of metal above the quarter glass opening. This section of metal did not fit the curvature of my new roofline and had to be removed. Later, once I have completed welding the door posts and reshaping the quarter glass openings, I'll shape a patch that better suits my needs and cover this opening.

Moving slightly toward the rear of the car, notice the pair of Vise-Grip pliers in photo 14, holding the sail panel to the roof panel. To get this overlap of metal, I had to physically push the sail panel area inboard and clamp it into place.

PHOTO 12: Using the template shown in photo 8, I can now mark the top of the door frame for cutting.

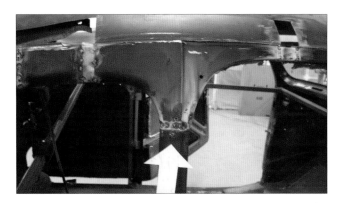

PHOTO 13: The top of the center door post has been moved back to align with the lower door post. Notice the gap in the roof panel created by this move.

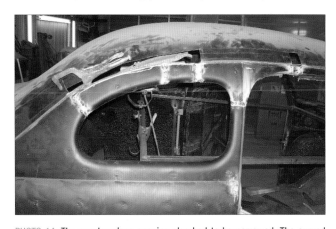

PHOTO 14: The quarter glass opening also had to be narrowed. The curved upper half of the opening had to be cut apart and repositioned to retain that natural curve of the opening.

This push inboard was necessary to retain that gentle sweep of the roofline. I'll use blind holders to hold the roof panel and sail panel together, then tack weld along the slit to help hold things together.

Of course, everything you've seen here has to be duplicated on the other side of the car. The good news is that now you know exactly what has to be done and you have a prime example to copy.

NOTES

NOTES

CHAPTER 9

COMPLETING
THE TOP CHOP

With most of the major modifications to the top chop completed, I decide to spend some quality time with the Eastwood Planishing Hammer Kit #28116. I need to shape out a couple of new metal sections to fill the voids I've created just above the quarter glass surround structure on both sides of the car (photo 1).

FILLING THE VOIDS WITH SHAPED METAL

The Eastwood Planishing Hammer is the ideal tool for this job, as the patch panels I need to make have compound curves and would otherwise require a lot of hammer and dolly work to get the right shape. The patch you can see in photo 2 took about thirty minutes to form using the planishing hammer.

Other things going on in photo 2 that you should be aware of include the use of blind holders, Eastwood Panel Holding System #19074, to hold the patch panel in place. Notice also that the patch covers a much larger area than the actual gap created when I pulled the roof panel forward (photo 3). If I were repairing a rust hole, I would be more inclined to size the patch to fit the repair. But in this case, I'm dealing with joining two different panels, the roof and the upper quarter glass structure, and both have very different curvatures. This is a result of having moved the roof forward. If I attempted to fill only the existing void of

metal with a new patch, the resulting repair would be shaped more like a pumpkin and not at all like a gently curved roofline. I need the gently curved roofline to keep the shape and flow of this car looking right. The best way to ensure that this is exactly what I get is to form a patch panel that is at least twice as large as the void being filled.

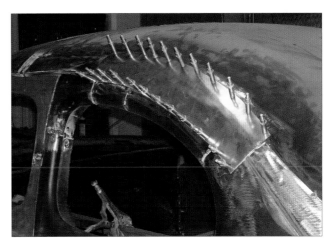

PHOTO 2: The first patch panel gets a test fitting before the roof and upper quarter glass opening are flanged to accept the piece.

PHOTO 1: A planishing hammer is used to shape the patch panels needed to reshape the roof just above the quarter glass openings.

PHOTO 3: This is the actual hole being covered by the patch panel. Notice that this hole is much smaller than the patch being used to cover it.

Of course, once I'm happy with the shape and the fit of the new panel, I'll enlarge the hole under the patch, flange the edges to give the patch a better fit, then weld it solid. What does it look like when completed? Glad you asked. Check out photo 4.

REMOVING THE DRIP RAILS

If you refer back to photo 2, you will see this car no longer has drip rails. In keeping with one of my original ideas for the build of this car, to remove everything on the exterior that might detract from its sleek looks, the drip rails had to go. To facilitate removal, I used a pneumatic die grinder with a 3-inch cutoff wheel attached, and I removed the rails flush with the body. That left a seam to deal with, as the drip rails were sandwiched between the roof panel and the quarter panels. When time allows, I'll weld these seams solid. For now, I need to move on to the doors.

IF THE DOORS DON'T FIT

I'll begin by ensuring the fit of my freshly chopped doors. I cut the tops off of both doors in the last chapter. That lets me open and close the doors without them bumping into the chopped roof panel. Who cares if the doors can be opened or closed at this point in the repair? Recall that I said cutting loose the windshield and door posts often results in the body springing apart due to the stresses on the metal? Now is a good time to be sure the body is still square and true and that both doors still fit the door openings.

You might say I got lucky in that the doors fit perfectly. But I say luck had nothing to do with it. I braced this body thoroughly, therefore I expected the doors to open and close exactly as they had prior to cutting the top loose. OK, I realize things not only *can* go wrong, quite often they *do* go wrong. Let's assume the right door no longer fits the way it should. The gap seems oddly wide at the front, particularly up near the windshield post. Where do you go to find the problem? Look no farther than the windshield post. Because the door is now rear hinged, the windshield post is the only place where things could have gone wrong to cause the door gap to widen.

Wait a minute. Am I saying a wide gap at the cowl, or windshield post, is the only problem that could

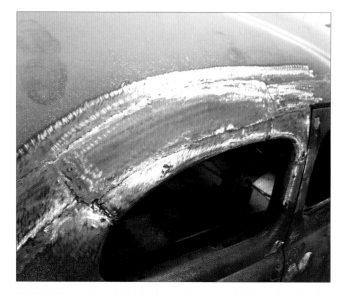

PHOTO 4: The result of all this shaping and forming and fitting and welding is a gently sloping roofline. This is going to keep the flow of the car moving in the right direction.

exist with the fit of the doors? Pretty much. That is, unless you hacked your ride apart without bothering to brace the body at all, and if that is the case, I can't help you unless you bring me the car and a great big pile of money.

Anyway, if the gap is too wide at the front of the door, the solution is to first cut loose the added cowl bracing that extends along the length of the body. Leave any other added bracing in place. What has happened is that the body sprang apart once the windshield posts were cut loose. It is a little uncommon and is usually due to poor welding techniques or, as I said before, to the failure to properly brace the body. The trick now is to take the spring out of it.

Use a ratcheting cable puller and hook one end to the cowl. Use "C" clamp–style Vise-Grip pliers if necessary to give you a place to hook the cable puller. Now hook the other end of the puller to a point near the floor as far back in the car as possible. Apply tension to the puller and the door gap should close nicely. Weld additional bracing inside the car to hold the body rigid.

The cowl didn't move when you tried to pull it back using the ratcheting cable puller? You will need to cut the tack welds on the windshield post where the roof was chopped, pull the cowl back, then tack weld the post again.

With that out of the way it's time to get back to completing the doors.

WRAPPING UP THE CHOPS

Previously, I removed the tops of the door window frames so they could be chopped to fit the new roofline. I started by making templates of the tops of the doors to help determine where to make my cuts. After that, I removed the upper door frames from the doors by cutting them into two separate sections. Refer back to the previous chapter if you need more information on how I removed the tops of the doors.

The cuts were made basically the same way I cut the door posts and windshield posts—by first wrapping the cut lines with ¾-inch-wide masking tape to ensure that my cuts were straight, then by making the cuts using a reciprocating saw with a metal cutting blade attached. I removed a 3-inch-long section from the rear window glass frame of the door and a 3⅛-inch-long section from the front window glass frame. Why the addition ⅛ inch difference? The front window glass frame is slanted slightly rearward. The extra ⅛ inch compensates for that slant.

Check out photo 5 for a look at the finished product. Here you can see where I removed the 3-inch section from the rear door window frame and butted the two pieces back together. Notice also that the cut line on the door window frame is a few inches below the cut line where I lowered the roof panel at the center door post. I deliberately staggered these cut points so that I would have good alignment points to use as comparison to ensure that the joining points are perfectly straight.

While we are here at photo 5, also notice the small section of metal added at the top center of the door window frame. The width of this section of metal is the same as the width of metal used to span the gap in the roof panel at the point where I moved the upper portion of the center door post back.

Anything else? Not really. The roof is chopped, the doors are chopped, the quarter glass openings are chopped, and everything fits and is in good alignment overall. The only thing remaining is to spend a few hours welding each and every seam and butt joint, using the MIG welder.

CHOPPING THE GARNISH MOLDINGS

Next on the "gotta get it done" list are the garnish moldings. I'll start by refreshing your knowledge of moldings. If a molding is mounted on the exterior of a vehicle, that molding is typically referred to as a reveal molding. If a molding is mounted on the interior of a vehicle, that molding is typically referred to as a garnish molding.

Refer to photo 6 for a look at my goal. If you chop the doors, you also have to chop the garnish moldings around the windows. In this car, that would include chopping the garnish moldings for both of the door glass openings, both quarter window openings, and the windshield opening. The size of the back glass was not altered, so the original garnish molding will still fit this opening.

Refer to photo 7 to see how the chop was made. I'll describe my work on the left door, as the techniques used here are the same as those required for all of the other glass openings. Notice that I've already cut the garnish molding in half and have positioned the lower piece in place on the door. The arrow points

PHOTO 5: Here is a look at the completed chop on the left door window opening frame.

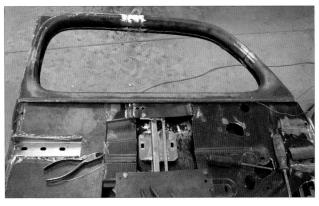

PHOTO 6: The garnish moldings surrounding the windows and windshield also need to be chopped. Here is the chopped garnish molding installed on the left door.

to the ¾-inch-wide masking tape wrapped around the door window frame opening. The tape is there to mark the point where I cut the garnish molding.

Now refer to photo 8. I've removed the lower piece of garnish molding and positioned the top half of the garnish molding in place on the door. It isn't obvious here, but Ford used trim screws to attach all of their garnish moldings. I'll take advantage of that by

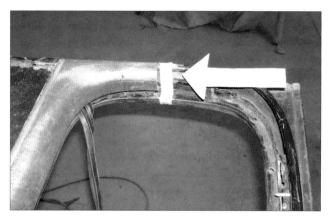

PHOTO 7: Masking tape is used to define the cut line for the lower half of the garnish molding.

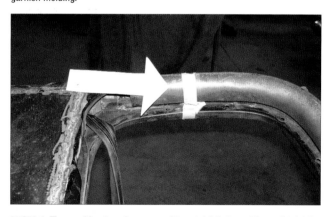

PHOTO 8: The masking tape is now used to establish the cutting point for the upper half of the garnish molding.

securing my molding pieces in place with trim screws. Screwing the moldings down ensures that they are in the correct location on the door.

Using the masking tape line as a reference point, I added another length of masking tape to the upper half of the molding above the first tape line. Why? This gives me a perfect cut line for chopping the top half of the garnish molding.

Once all of my cuts have been made and the pieces have been fitted together, I again secure the garnish moldings to the door with screws before welding.

PICKING A POWER WINDOW UNIT

As long as I'm working on the doors, this is a good time to add a little power to the windows. I don't think I mentioned this aspect of the build before, but the plan calls for eliminating the door vent windows. That calls for having new door glasses cut to fit the much larger window openings created by eliminating the vent windows and, of course, some way to lift and lower the new windows once they are mounted in the doors.

Out in the world of aftermarket parts, all types of universal power door glass regulators can be found. Of those, I have a choice between plastic drive actuators and cable drive actuators that do the actual lifting and lowering of the glass. Having changed out enough broken plastic drive ribbons used in some factory actuators to lift and lower the door glasses, I've become a little leery of those types of regulators. I opt instead for cable drive units like the one shown in photo 9.

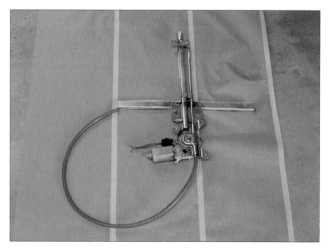

PHOTO 9: The left door power window unit I'll be installing in the car.

PHOTO 10: The completed power window installation.

This unit comes in kit form with everything that's needed to complete the installation, including the wiring and switches. I'll deal with the wiring aspect later. Right now, I need to find a way to install this unit in my door.

INSTALLING THE POWER UNIT

Photo 10 gives you an idea of where I'm headed with this installation. First, notice that I removed a large section of metal from the center of the inner door frame and replaced it with a large, flat plate made from 16-gauge steel. Notice also that the plate is bolted to the door and not welded. The plate serves one function: to provide a flat surface to mount the power regulator. The plate is removable because otherwise I wouldn't have the room to get the regulator inside the door.

Finally, notice the chipboard template serving as a temporary door glass. A little later in this build, I'll have my glass guy come out and measure the car for new windows and a new windshield. This template will help him figure out what size to cut the new door glasses, and in the meantime it will help me figure out how to mount the regulator.

ONE STEP AT A TIME

Here's the process. The new power regulator must be centered in the door as well as on the door glass to prevent the glass from rocking and jamming as it is rolled up.

The next step is to make the door glass template. I started with a cardboard template, then transferred that to the more sturdy chipboard template shown in the photo.

If you look closely at photo 10, you can just see the rubber weather stripping around the glass opening. This weather stripping is from Steele Rubber Products and is the same size and style of the weather stripping Ford originally used to seal the door glasses.

> ### TIP
>
> *Here are a few tips. If the template binds at any point while it is being moved up or down, it will need to be shaved for a better fit. If the template rocks or seems loose in the run channels, it is too small, and a slightly larger template should be tested. Wonder why chipboard comes in 4 x 8 sheets? You'll understand once you've fabricated a door glass template—or two, or three.*

Having the weather stripping in place is a must in order to correctly size the glass template.

Now I need run channels for the glass. The rear run channel is already in the door, so it will be used. I fabricated the front run channel using the run channel from the discarded vent glass assembly. The only thing of note here is that the position of the front run channel is dictated by the width of the new door glass. Of course, the width of the new door glass can be determined only by fabricating a template and carefully fitting it into the weather stripping. Yep, this takes time. The template must move easily up and down the new run channels and slip snugly into the weather stripping around the top of the door. By the way, the run channels must be mounted parallel to each other with enough space between them for the glass and the weather stripping.

The last step is to temporarily mount the glass template to the glass guide on the power regulator. I drill a couple of holes through the guide and secure the template with screws. To make sure that everything works as I had planned, I check the operation of the power unit by attaching a battery charger to the motor and moving the glass template up and down a few times.

A FLIP-DOWN LICENSE PLATE DOOR

While I'm in the powering up mode, I had an idea for constructing a flip-down door for the rear license plate. Call me unconventional, but I never liked the flip-up rear license plate bracket that seems so popular on the older rides these days. I want to fabricate a license plate housing, inset it into the rear body panel, then construct a movable door that flips up to hide the license plate when the car is parked and flips down to display the plate once the engine is started.

Photo 11 shows my housing. I started the same way I've started just about every other aspect of this build: by first making a cardboard template, then using the template to cut, fold, and shape the actual housing. The template is just visible near the top of the photograph.

I really don't like to show the seriously ugly shots such as photo 12 that I take during mock-up, but sometimes I think it can be helpful to see the tribula-

PHOTO 11: The rear license plate housing. This piece will be inset into the rear body panel.

PHOTO 12: The new flip-down license plate pocket tack welded into place. Yep, it's ugly, but getting better.

tions car nuts go through as they take an idea from head scratching to reality. What I've done here is tack welded the housing into the rear body panel, then fabricated a door to fit over the housing. This door will eventually flip down to expose the license plate.

Photo 13 shows the final mock-up. I've added a license lamp to the door to illuminate the plate as well as stop plates at the upper corners of the pocket. I'll drill these plates to accept rubber bumpers to prevent the door from banging against the pocket as it closes.

Further down the road I'll also add an electric motor to the door so that it automatically opens when the engine is started and automatically closes when the engine is shut off.

PHOTO 13: A shot with the flip-down door open. Notice the license lamp attached to the door.

NOTES

CHAPTER 10

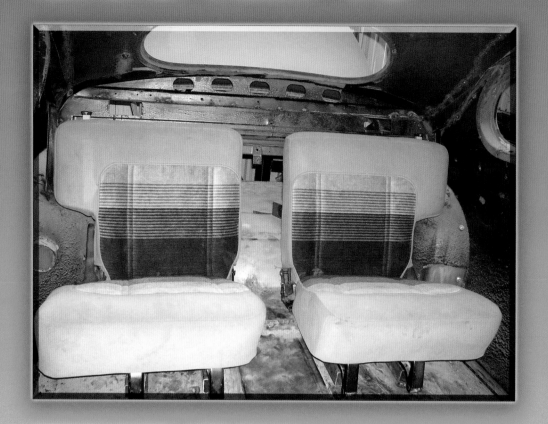

TIME FOR
SEATS, AC, AND
A BRAKE PEDAL

This chapter is going to cover a lot of ground, sort of a catchall chapter designed to touch on a lot of details that are often overlooked when it comes to building a vehicle. For instance, where will the seats mount? Will they allow the driver to comfortably reach the brake pedal? What about that brake pedal? Where and how will it be mounted? Then don't forget about the AC. A closed cabin street rod needs both a heater and an air conditioner. Like I said, it's the details that make for a nice ride, and none of them can be overlooked.

SEAT SELECTION

Starting first with the interior of the car, I need to mount the seats. Originally, this car had a single bench seat up front with a platform in the rear seat area designed for carrying salesmen's sample cases. Sample cases were far too important and valuable to just be tossed into the trunk. They required special handling, so that meant carrying them in the car with the driver.

I'm not a salesman, so I don't carry around samples of my work. I may drive a sample occasionally, but that's another story altogether. Having no samples to deal with frees up the space behind the front seat for the addition of a rear seat. But what seat? A check into the aftermarket world of seating reveals an absolute feast of seating possibilities, ranging from the bland type of bench seating resembling the original seats that came with the car to top of the line heated, vibrating, body wrapping, automatic adjusting, leather-bound custom-made bucket seats.

I already knew bench seating was out. I had designed this car with bucket seats in mind, and because of the way I constructed the driveshaft tunnel to accept a console, there was no turning back. That was about the time that fate intervened, and my seating dilemma settled itself. I had just darkened the gate of my favorite salvage yard, excuse me, automotive reclamation center, and was almost run down by a tow truck delivering a cracked up late model Ford Explorer, complete with pristine seats. For less than $100, I drove away from the center with two

excellent front bucket seats, two outstanding fold-down rear seats, and a full set of seat belts that are going to look great in the '46.

But don't think I watched that bent-up chunk of Explorer roll past me and instantly decided those were the seats for me. I had already taken several measurements inside the '46 and had a pretty good idea of which seats would and would not fit the car. The Explorer's seats fell neatly into the measurement range I had previously calculated.

INSTALLING THE NEW SEATS

So how do you remove seats from one vehicle and transplant them into another vehicle? Actually, it is pretty easy. You pay attention to the shape of the floor in the donor vehicle. The manufacturers don't put humps and bumps in their floor pans just for the sake of adding humps and bumps. Each one is there for a reason and serves a specific purpose, such as a means by which the seats can be mounted. In this case, the rear fold-down seats require platforms to elevate the seat cushions and angled brackets for mounting the outside swivels on the seat backs. The front seats need an elevated platform for the front mounts and a level area for the rear mounts. Nothing to it.

I start my installation with the rear seats (photo 1). The elevated platforms for the seat cushions (lower arrow) are constructed of 2 x 2-inch square steel tubing. To mount the seat cushions to the platforms, I drill two

$\frac{7}{16}$-inch holes in each platform, then weld $\frac{3}{8}$-inch nuts over each hole on the inside of the tubing. I do the same thing to the angled seat-back bracket (upper arrow) and to the floor pan, where the inside seat-back bracket mounts. What's the mounting angle of the outside swivel mount? That would be about 30 degrees.

To add extra strength to the inside seat-back mounts, I cut two 4 x 4-inch square plates from a sheet of $\frac{3}{16}$-inch-thick steel and tack weld those plates to the underside of the floor pan. Once the seats are in the car, I'll use bolts long enough to extend down through the reinforcing plates and add large flat washers and nuts to better secure the seats. Why go to all of the trouble? The inner seat belts also mount to this bracket. The addition of the

plates will ensure that the mounting bolts cannot be pulled out in the event of an accident (photo 2).

Yes, adding these plates under the floor pan means I'll be threading bolts through the nuts that I've already welded to the floor pan in the passenger compartment and extending them far enough through the floor to add flat washers and additional nuts. This was an easy way to elevate the inner seat brackets by $\frac{1}{2}$ inch, which I needed to do to keep the seat backs perfectly level.

What's the strange-looking addition to the rear wheel well visible in photo 1? Check out photo 3, and you will see that the rear seats are contoured to fit around the wheel wells on the Explorer. The wheel wells on the '46 sit farther back in the car, so I fabricated extra wells to fill the void created by the seats. Once these wells are covered with upholstery and carpeted, they will blend perfectly into the interior and will give the illusion of actual wheel wells.

The front seats are a little easier to install. Up here, all I need is a couple of platforms for the front seat mounts. The rear mounts will bolt directly through the floor pan and into one of the steel bracing bars added prior to installing the new floor pans. I fabricated the platforms from 16-gauge steel, and each one measures 13 inches long by 2 inches tall by 2 inches wide. Again, I drill the platforms and weld nuts to the inside of the pieces to make bolting the seats to the platforms that much easier.

To determine exactly where the front seats are to be mounted, I position the driver's seat in the car, climb into the car, and shut the door. I want the seat close enough to the door to make it comfortable to rest my arm on a proposed armrest, but not so close that the door actually touches the seat. In this case, the gap between the seat and the door is about 4 inches.

PHOTO 1: To mount the rear seats, I needed two things. The upper arrow points to the angled bracket for the outside seat back mount. The lower arrow points to the 2 x 2–inch steel tubing used to fabricate the rear seat cushion mounts.

PHOTO 2: A view of the reinforcing plate I'll add to the underside of the floor pan to better anchor the seat belts.

PHOTO 3: Notice the contoured area on the outside of the seat back. To maintain a natural look, I constructed a fake wheel well just in front of the rear one.

But that's not all. The seat must also be centered with the steering wheel. That means temporarily installing the dash and steering column. I use the old dash as a template and have my trusty assistant, Bryan, do his contortionist act to hold the steering column in place while I pretend to cruise down the highway at 80. I liked the seat right where it sat, which was 21 inches back from the firewall and 5 inches inboard of the rocker panel, as measured from the front seat mounting platform.

SEAT BELTS

That leaves one safety item to contend with: the front seat belts. Like the rear seat belts, the inner seat belts on the front seats are attached to the seat frames. That means that the seat belts are only as secure as the seats. To ensure that the seats are securely mounted in the car, I position the front seat rear mounting bolts so that they could be bolted directly through the 1-inch-wide steel bar I welded underneath the floor pan back when I installed the new floor pans.

The outside seat belts are the three-point-style belts that came in the donor Explorer. To mount these belts, I bolt the retractor units to the steel reinforcing bars used to secure the door hinges on either side of the car (photo 4). The opposite end of the belts will use the same mounting point. The upper mounts, where the belts loop up to drape over the shoulder when fastened (photo 5), are located just behind the upper door openings.

THE MECHANICALS

With the seating arrangements settled, I turn my attention to filling the dash area with all sorts of mechanical gizmos, including a hanging brake pedal assembly, steering column, windshield wiper motor, and heater/air conditioner unit.

THE HEATER/AIR CONDITIONER

Wait a minute. Doesn't the plan call for mounting the AC unit behind the rear seat? Yes, it did. That was part of the reason I constructed the driveshaft tunnel the way I did, to accommodate the plumbing necessary to achieve that goal. But if most good body men have only one decent quality about them, it is the ability to listen to and then implement ideas and suggestions from people who have already been there.

The point is that when I called Hot Rod Air to order up a quality AC system for the '46, my brain was treated to a very informative discussion about where best to locate the AC unit in the car. Here are a few details you might find useful. The '46 is a big car. Heating this car could be easily achieved from a unit mounted just about anywhere. However, I want a defroster in this car. That's when the problems associated with rear-mounted heaters began to rear their ugly heads. The guys at Hot Rod Air left me with no doubt that air could be moved from the rear of the car to the windshield, but most of the heat would be lost in the process.

Anyone who has ever tested a defroster with a hand knows it takes warm air, and a lot of it, to defrost a windshield. Piping air all the way from behind the rear seat to the windshield would result in tepid air at best. This slightly warm air would have very little chance at actually warming the windshield. Actual defrosting just wasn't going to happen. Strike one.

PHOTO 4: The seat belt retractor unit is bolted to the same steel bar used to secure the door hinges. I'll use the same mounting point for the opposite end of the seat belt.

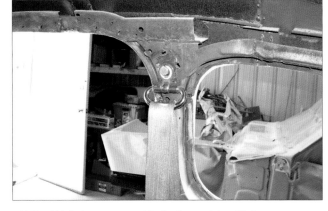

PHOTO 5: This is the upper mount for the three-point seat belts.

Next is the problem of delivering cold air from the rear of the car up to the dash panel in the front. Did you know that the air in a typical AC vent can be as much as 10 degrees warmer as it exits the vent than it was when it left the AC unit that's mounted only a few inches away? Project a loss like that over the several feet of vent hose needed to pipe cool air from the rear to the front, and it is strike two.

Finally, where do the AC vents point? They don't point at your feet like the heater vents or to the roof like the defroster vents. They point directly at you. That's because the AC unit is working best when it is directly cooling the vehicle occupants. On a hot day, I don't care if the carpet or the headliner is cool. I want the cool air blowing on me. Make sense? So strike three, and the rear-mounted unit is out.

So how does the new heater/AC unit fit under the dash (photo 6)? Obviously, the compact design makes this the perfect unit for my needs. The ducts will be easy to route, the lines easy to attach, and what really makes this unit worth its weight is I still have room for a glove box. How long did it take to mount this part of the system? About three minutes.

When I get a little further down the road with this project, I'll unpack the rest of the goodies that came in the Hot Rod Air kit and go through the entire installation procedure. But just in case you are wondering, the kit contains everything needed to add heating and air conditioning to any ride, including the louvered vents needed to direct all that cold air directly at you.

STEERING

The next things on my punch list for installation include the steering column, hanging brake pedal assembly, and windshield wiper assembly. I'll start with the steering column.

My steering column came from an early '80s GM product, possibly a Camaro, as the column is a tilt column without the column shift. This column was part of the package deal when I purchased the car, and I would hate to give it the toss. The only problem I have with the column is that I prefer not to have a column-mounted ignition key, so the first step is to disassemble the column and remove the ignition switch and steering lock mechanism.

The steering lock mechanism consists of a steel shaft that slides up to engage a locking ring on the column

PHOTO 6: The main unit of the Hot Rod Air system is mounted under the dash. The unit is compact and will take up very little of the precious space behind the dash.

shaft when the key is turned to the lock position. I remove the shaft along with the ignition switch.

After that, I grind away the ignition switch "bump" from the column and fill the opening with epoxy. A little body work and paint will make this column look like new and leave everyone guessing as to its origin.

PUTTING ON THE BRAKES

One thing I did toss out with the old rusted parts was the frame-mounted brake pedal assembly. Stomping on the brake pedal just isn't ergonomically correct, so I opted to install a hanging brake pedal assembly. Once again, browsing the aftermarket parts catalogs yielded several hanging brake configurations, and after turning a few dozen pages, I settled on a Wilwood unit that will allow me to hide the brake master cylinder under the dash just above the brake pedal. That will keep the firewall clean, and for me that's a big plus.

Mounting this unit requires a little up-front planning, as the foot room in the car is somewhat suspect. I've driven old rides in the past that had the gas pedal mounted up on the driveshaft hump in order to make room for the steering column and brake pedal. That positioning may be OK for a short drive to the show and shine meet, but it can become very tedious on a long trek.

I've also driven old rides that had the brake and gas pedals crammed so close together that pressing on one meant pressing on the other. That's no way to drive a car either. My solution was to mount the gas pedal in a comfortable position just to the left of the driveshaft tunnel, then mount the hanging brake pedal on the left side of the steering column. I know what you are thinking, that's where the clutch pedal goes. You're right, but in this case moving the pedal to the other side of the steering column let me move the gas pedal farther to the left. That makes it far more comfortable to press and keeps the brake pedal far enough away from the gas pedal so as not to risk pressing both pedals at the same time. There is still plenty of room to the left of the brake pedal so that it doesn't seem as if your left foot should be pressing the pedal, and the entire setup has a good feel to it.

WIPING UP MY MESSES

With a steering column, brake pedal assembly, and heater unit now tucked under the dash, finding space for the wiper motor suddenly becomes a challenge (photo 7). Here is a shot of the left side of the dash area.

Once again, what you are seeing is this car in the raw stages of mock-up. First, notice the brackets used to mount the hanging brake pedal and the steering column. All of the brackets are made from 1-inch square steel tubing. If anything at all needs to be said about this setup, it is that all of these brackets must be securely welded once they are in their final positions. That means I should be able to reach an engine hoist into the car and use these brackets to lift the front of this body off the frame without damaging anything!

So how does everything mount? Check out photo 8. Again, what you are seeing is rough mock-up work, but you get the idea. Everything is in its place. Everything has room to function properly, and, most important of all, everything can be accessed even after the dash panel has been installed.

PHOTO 7: The left side of the dash area. Visible are the brackets used to hang the brake pedal and steering column, and just to the right of the brackets hangs the wiper motor assembly. This is the mock-up stage, so notice the lengthened wiper shaft leading to the right wiper arm.

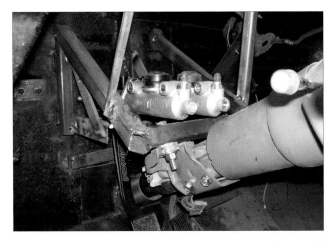

PHOTO 8: The left side of the dash with the steering column and brake pedal assembly mounted.

NOTES

NOTES

CHAPTER 11

THE FIRST PROJECT MOCK-UP

This will be my first opportunity to mock up this car completely. I've had the doors and the deck lid mounted, but up until now I haven't had a chance to mount any of the front sheet metal or the rear fenders.

Mostly, I just want to be sure everything fits. Fenders, including the rear ones, on old rides like this can be very troublesome to mount and align. Then there is the hood. Often these panels are in a world of their own when it comes to fitting. They have a way of looking perfectly straight and true when lying on the bench, yet once mounted on the car, they can fit like, well, like they were never meant to be mounted in the first place. Toss into that mix the question of whether the hood hinges are in good working order, and the need to hang some sheet metal becomes very apparent.

BUILDING A LAND SHARK

So what does this huge boat look like when assembled? Check out photo 1. This should also answer any lingering questions concerning my decision to chop the top. I can only imagine what a bubble top–looking ride this would have been with the stock roofline. But that's not why I mocked up the car. I hung the additional sheet metal to check the panel-to-panel alignment. That proved to be much better than anticipated, so that left me with free time to ponder another issue: the final stance of the car. If you look closely at photo 1, you will notice I've already removed a couple of inches of metal from the bottom of the leading edges of the front fenders. Isn't it funny how free time often leads to more work?

I'll go through the process of performing this cutaway job in a moment, but before I do, let me explain that I removed 2 inches to kill that straight line look along the bottom of the car. That should improve on the stance of the car by giving it more of a shark nose appearance. It should also help nullify some of that huge, flat shape around the grille area. Where's the bumper? It's collecting dust somewhere in storage. It's not going back on the car. It would greatly detract from the look I'm going for.

CHOPPING THE FENDERS

Photo 2 shows the right fender. My first step is to measure 1½ inches up from the bottom of the fender and place a mark at several points across the front of the fender. Next, I join the marks using masking tape to lay out my first cut line. This line travels from the inside corner of the fender where it meets the grille, around to the sides, then gently sweeps up as it meets the wheel opening. I'll remove the lower part of the fender along the cut line

PHOTO 1: The '46 with all of its panels in place for the first time. Yep, it's a big car, but it's going to look nice!

using a die grinder, then set this part of the fender aside. I'll need it later.

I measure up another 2 inches, make a few more marks, then lay out another cut line using the ¾-inch-wide masking tape as a guide. This cut is also made using the die grinder with a 3-inch cutoff wheel attached. Don't forget the safety equipment: eye protection, ear protection, and heavy gloves.

PHOTO 2: Here, 1½ inches of the fender have been removed with a die grinder.

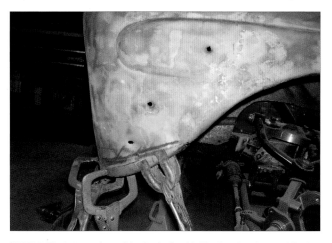

PHOTO 3: The bottom piece of the fender is added back to the shortened fender.

PHOTO 4: The end result after the bottom edge of the fender is reattached. The fender is shorter but still looks factory.

Remember the lower fender piece I removed earlier? Now I'm ready to install it back on the fender (photo 3). I've switched to the left fender for a better view, so look closely and you'll see the piece is no longer 1½ inches wide; now it is only about 1 inch wide. What was that all about? Cutting the piece 1½ inches wide gave me room to adjust the piece up and down on the bottom of the fender until I achieved what I thought would be the perfect position. That proved to be higher than first thought, so I reduced the width of the piece by ½ inch. Getting rid of ½ inch also made reshaping the piece to fit the fender a little easier. Once satisfied with the shape and the fit of the piece, I flanged the bottom edge of the fender using Eastwood Panel Flanger #31092 to give me a flush fit. Vise-Grip pliers hold the piece in place on the fender for welding.

Photo 4 shows the result. In a nutshell, I simply moved the bottom of the fender up by a couple of inches so that the fender doesn't hang so low in the front. I was also careful to retain the gentle curve of the wheel opening to keep the look natural. Not bad.

THE TAILLIGHTS

The last major modification to be made to this car concerns the taillights. In keeping with the theme of shaving and smoothing this car, I can't leave the taillights bulging from the rear fenders. They need to be "Frenched." What does that mean?

Photo 5 shows the final result in mock-up. Notice that the taillight has been recessed into the fender. That's known as Frenching. OK, Frenching is a term normally associated with creating an eyebrow over the headlights. In this case, my eyebrow is located vertically and on the inboard side of the taillights.

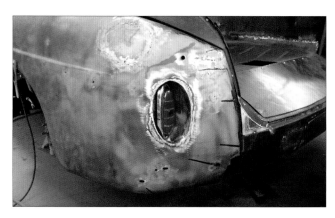

PHOTO 5: The taillights are Frenched into the fenders, in keeping with the smooth look of the car.

The process starts with a cardboard template of the taillight housings that is cut ¼ inch larger than the housing itself. What taillights did I use? These are stock 1946 Ford taillights mounted vertically instead of horizontally. It's not my fault that Ford originally got the mounting wrong.

The extra ¼ inch around the template gives me a little bit of gap all around the taillight once it has been inset into the fender. This is necessary since some wiggle room is needed to get the taillight into and out of the mounting pocket without worry of scratching the paint.

The template also has to be placed perfectly vertical on the fender, another reason for mocking up the car and mounting all four fenders. I can't have the taillights mounted crooked or leaning off toward the back forty.

In photo 6, you can see I've removed the fender from the car and laid out the opening for cutting. To make locating the cut lines a little easier, I use masking tape to help highlight where the fender is to be cut. I'll use a die grinder with a 3-inch cutoff wheel attached to make the cut. Where did I locate the hole on the fender? This is an eyeball thing. I taped the template to the fender while it was still mounted on the car, moved it around, and arrived at what I thought was the best location. That happens to be 6 inches outboard of the deck lid opening and 8 inches up from the bottom of the fender. What's the tape line through the center of the template used for? This is my vertical locator to help keep the template straight up and down.

Photo 7 shows all of the pieces. The stock 1946 Ford taillight assembly is there to be sure that my new mounting pocket is the correct size. I've also got a completed mounting pocket and the components for making the other mounting pocket. Those components consist of an oval plate I made using the template of the housing and a rectangular piece measuring 3½ x 18 inches. The oval piece will become the base-plate, and the rectangular piece will be curved around it to form the pocket. Both pieces are made from 16-gauge steel.

About the only thing you can't tell from here is that the base-plate must be arched a little to conform to the shape of the stock taillight housing. One thing you can tell if you look closely is that I cut a square opening in the base-plate for the lamp housing to protrude through.

The new pocket is a perfect fit (photo 8). Notice that I inset the pocket so that the inside edge is flush with the fender. That leaves the outside edge of the pocket protruding from the fender by 2¾ inches. This is basically what accomplishes the French effect. I'll finish this installation by tack welding the pocket to the fender. After that, I need to be sure the taillight is perfectly vertical. I don't want the light shining up, down, or out to the back forty.

PHOTO 6: Every operation starts with a template. The line down the center of the template helps me locate the piece absolutely vertical on the fender. The masking tape identifies where the cuts will be made.

PHOTO 7: The pieces making up the Frenched taillight pocket include a base-plate and a rectangular plate that will be wrapped around the base-plate to form the new taillight pocket.

PHOTO 8: The new taillight pocket is tack welded to the fender. Notice that the inside of the pocket is flush with the fender and the outside protrudes several inches from the fender. The excess metal will be trimmed away later.

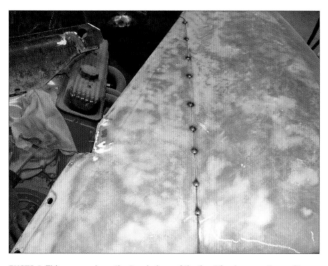

PHOTO 9: This seam where the two halves of the front fenders meet wasn't necessary. I decided to eliminate it by welding it solid.

It must shine straight back. I'll use a small carpenter's square with a level to be sure the pocket is mounted nice and straight in the fender. Once that is done, I can cut away the excess metal from the pocket and bring it flush with the fender all around. Then, it is a matter of welding the pocket solid to the fender and grinding the welds smooth, which brings me back to photo 5, the end result.

Something not so obvious about this modification is that the taillight lens actually extends past the edge of the fender by about ¼ inch. This was intentional. I automatically ended up with a side marker lamp by allowing the side of the taillight to be seen from the side of the car. This is a safety factor that was very easy to incorporate into the assembly and still retain the smooth, flowing look I want for the car.

FILLING THE COWL VENT

Originally the taillights were the last major modifications planned for the car. But, as with every other car I've ever worked on, I always make one last trip around it wondering and pondering if this is the place to stop. In this case, I decide upon two additional changes. Both are very simple, and both are very much needed to complete the look of this car.

First, I remove the cowl vent assembly and weld a steel plate over the opening. Fresh air will have to be introduced into the car from some other point, and when I make that decision I'll let you know. Second, and this one has already raised the eyebrows of a few car builder friends, I weld the top seam on both front fenders closed (photo 9). You can see I've only tack welded the fenders at this point, but you get the idea. No more seam line on top of the fenders.

THE FIRST COAT OF EPOXY

At last that brings me to a long awaited point in this build. Yesteryear, I would have told you the car is leaving surgery and moving into recovery. But this isn't a restoration, it's a build, so you never know. I might change my mind at any point and once again subject the car to some type of metal replacement surgery; but as for right now, no more surgery. It is time for recovery.

That starts by once again sanding the exterior of the car from top to bottom. The sandpaper of choice is 80 grit, and I'll use everything from a hand sanding pad to a pneumatic orbital sander to roughen up the Eastwood Rust Encapsulator applied previously to keep surface rust at bay.

After sanding, it is on to the epoxy coat. The epoxy of choice is House of Kolor KP2CF part A & B (photo 10). This is an epoxy-based primer/surfacer that mixes at a 1:1 ratio. Application is two medium-wet coats using a Binks M1-G with a 1.4 mm spray tip.

It is a long way around this car with a spray gun (photo 11). I began spraying the roof, moved to the cowl, the right side, the rear of the car, and I am finishing on the left side. As you can see, I removed the front sheet metal before spraying. That allows me access to the cowl area and firewall to give that area a coat of epoxy. I didn't remove the rear fenders because I'm going to need them in place on the car to ensure that all points around the deck lid, rear fenders, and rear body panel end up flush and smooth once the plastic body filler has been applied.

Speaking of plastic body filler (photo 12), I'll skip ahead somewhat and offer this tip. Notice the door gap between the door and the quarter panel. When I began applying the plastic body filler to the sides of this car, I treated the door gaps as if they didn't exist. In other words, I smeared filler right over the gaps and filled them in. That allows me to treat the entire side of the car as a single panel instead of as two separate panels when it comes time for block sanding. The result is a perfect transition from panel to panel. Once I had the sides of the car sanded smooth, I used a die grinder with a 3-inch cutoff wheel to again open the door gaps. Nothing to it.

Now back to the initial epoxy coats. If this is your first time watching me reconstruct a car and you're wondering about this initial epoxy coat, let me explain. The paint manufacturers have figured out that applying a coat of epoxy does two things. First, it provides a very solid substrate over which all other refinishing products, including plastic body filler, can be applied. Second, it provides better adhesion and better moisture penetration control for any plastic body filler being applied to the car. That's the reasoning behind applying the epoxy coat but not the reason I'm addressing this part of the build at this point. I want to talk about the tools I'll be using for the next several weeks to give you the opportunity to go out and purchase them, if desired, before I get down to the dirty task of smoothing the sheet metal on this old ride.

To block sand the plastic body filler on any vehicle, you need four things. First, you need sandpaper. I start with 40 grit, move to 80 grit, then 100 grit, and finish with 180 grit.

Second, you need something to attach the sandpaper to in order to sand the car. I start with a pneumatic in-line sander and 40-grit sandpaper. This sander handles the rough sanding chores, as it begins the smoothing process by quickly locating any imperfections that might require additional filler or more hammer and dolly work.

Next, I move to hand sanding blocks. The rule is to use the longest block possible to sand a panel and always sand in an X pattern. For this car, I'll be using

PHOTO 10: The initial epoxy coat will come from House of Kolor, KP2CF A & B. This is an epoxy-based primer/surfacer used to prime the car prior to doing any plastic body filler repairs.

PHOTO 11: The car gets a single coat of epoxy.

three of Eastwood's adjustable flexible sanders: #31143, a 15-inch block; #31144, a 21-inch block; and #14283, a 27-inch sanding block. These are all fairly long blocks, but this is a big car, and big cars need long blocks.

So why these sanding blocks? To start with, they are made of urethane foam, which makes them easy to hold. Second, each block has three steel rods added to the foam to make the blocks rigid. That's great for flat surfaces, but when it comes to curved surfaces, the rods are removable to allow the blocks to better conform to the rounded surfaces. This car has lots of rounded surfaces, which means the steel rods will come and go as needed.

The third thing you need is a good guide coat. Try Eastwood #12389 Z. All this does is give the panel being sanded a contrasting topcoat that can be easily sanded off. The purpose of a guide coat is to let you see the condition of the surface being sanded and quickly locate any trouble spots. Any and all surface imperfections will collect and hold the guide coat and make them stand out so they can be dealt with.

How do you deal with minor imperfections? That brings me to the fourth thing you need, polyester putty. Basically, this is a thinned-down version of plastic body filler, and its purpose is to fill tiny imperfections in plastic body filler. For this car, I'll be using Evercoat Metal Glaze, Eastwood #31279 Z.

Did I say four things? Excuse me. Let's do five. Never, ever sand anything without a dust mask. Try a 3M #7048.

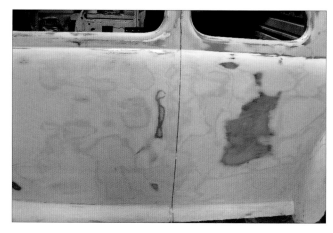

PHOTO 12: The sides of the car are treated as a single panel when applying body filler. Only after the filler has been sanded smooth do I cut open the door gap.

NOTES

_____

_____

_____

_____

_____

_____

_____

_____

_____

_____

_____

_____

NOTES

CHAPTER 12

WORKING WITH
BODY FILLER

Way back in my college days, I worked in a small body shop that specialized in street rods and fast cars. The owner of the shop insisted that I never apply body filler to any panel more than twice. That meant applying one coat of filler to take care of the waves and bumps in the metal and a second coat to take care of the minor imperfections, such as pinholes and deep scratches, left from sanding the first coat. I thought he was crazy, but it taught me the value of a good body hammer.

LESSONS LEARNED

As the years passed and I had opportunities to watch other body men ply their craft, it didn't take me long to learn that there are three types of body men: those who are part exchangers and can't repair metal, Bondo slingers who don't want to repair metal, and metal men. Metal men don't like to sling Bondo, much less sand it off once slung. They like to repair metal, then apply as little plastic body filler as possible in an effort to perfect the surface. I've always attempted to keep myself in the last category. I don't like sanding plastic body filler. The dust turns my hair white.

Unfortunately, it is practically impossible to build or restore a car today without the use of plastic body filler. Yes, there is lead repair. But working lead is an art within itself, and very few truly gifted lead workers are left in the world today. That's because working lead is hard on one's health, much more so than sanding plastic body filler, and is exceedingly hard on the pocketbook.

Yes, I hear it all the time, people don't want plastic body filler on their car. They think it won't hold up and will quickly crack and fall off. Well, it just ain't so. I've been at this for more than thirty years, and I've yet to have a vehicle return to the shop for additional repairs because the plastic body filler failed. I've repaired vehicles that were held together by plastic body filler because the metal has rusted away, but never the other way around. Plastic body filler is easy to work when being applied, strong when applied correctly, doesn't cost an arm and a leg, and, because of these reasons, is here to stay.

REMOVING BULLET DIMPLES

If you've tuned in to learn a few tidbits about how to massage metal, I hate to disappoint. The '46 really wasn't that beat up. I probably spent less than four hours with a body hammer in hand taking care of the dents and dings that were on the car. The car does have a few hundred bullet wounds, and a large number of them have resulted in small areas of stretched metal that need to be addressed. So I guess if I'm going to offer any tutorial at all on metal-working, it will be going through the fine art of removing bullet dimples without aggravating the already present stretched metal conditions.

> **TIP**
>
> *If you need in-depth information on removing dents and repairing sheet metal, refer to my book* Revive Your Ride: Secrets from a Body and Paint Restoration Pro; *it is packed with great information.*

Photo 1 shows a serious wound, maybe a .32 caliber at 20 yards. I can't simply place a dolly in front of this dimple and bang it flat from the backside using a body hammer. The metal is stretched. Attempting to bang it flat would stretch the metal even more, and that would result in a huge bubble of metal—not something I would like to see.

The solution is very simple (photo 2). Working from the back of the panel, I use a die grinder with a 3-inch cut-off wheel to cut an X in the bullet dimple. This gives all of the excess metal in the dimple a place to go when I hammer the dimple flat. Photo 3 shows the result. The dimple is gone, I've prevented the stretch of metal from spreading out over my panel, and all that is left to do is to MIG weld the cuts closed and grind everything smooth.

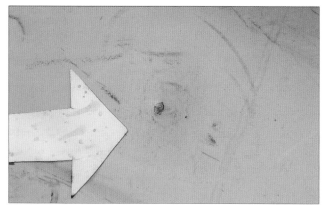

PHOTO 1: A long-standing custom out here in the back woods is to use old cars as target practice, which I'm guilty of perpetuating. Now it's time to reverse that trend and get rid of all the bullet dimples like this one.

PHOTO 2: I can't simply bang this dimple flat; too much stretched metal. The solution is to remove some of the excess metal by making an X cut across the dimple.

PHOTO 3: The excess metal had a place to go thanks to the X cuts. All that is left to do is to weld the cuts and grind the area smooth.

SANDING THE EPOXY COAT

With the bulk of my bumpy metal problems taken care of, I can now turn to making the body of this ride nice and smooth. That starts by sanding the epoxy coat. It is well cured and therefore needs to be roughed up before any plastic body filler can be applied. Since I applied two coats of epoxy, I have enough material on the car to let me get somewhat aggressive with the sanding. I'll use 180-grit sandpaper to sand the epoxy, and I'll employ everything from a handheld folded sheet of sandpaper to a soft foam hand sanding pad to sand every inch of this car. Once that's done, it is plastic body filler time.

Applying plastic body filler is pretty basic. I wear latex gloves to mix and apply the filler and use a 6-inch-wide plastic applicator to apply the coat as smoothly as possible.

I've been asked several times to explain my method of application and how I know my finished coats are rarely over $\frac{1}{4}$ inch thick. If you were standing next to me, this would take only a second, and you would be off and running. But you aren't here, so the best I can offer is to say that the thickness depends primarily on the position of the applicator during the application. The more vertically you hold the applicator, the thinner the coat. Holding the applicator at 75 degrees will result in an extremely thin and somewhat rough coat, while holding the applicator at 30 degrees will result in a thicker, smoother coat. That's the mechanics of applying filler, but getting the actual thickness you want requires practice.

If you have questions about the amount of filler being applied, try letting the filler cure and drilling into it at several locations to check the depth. Use a $\frac{3}{8}$-inch drill bit, and don't drill all the way through the panel. The drill will easily pass through the filler and stop when it touches the metal. Stop drilling at that point. Don't panic when you discover $\frac{1}{2}$ inch of depth prior to sanding. Sanding will easily remove $\frac{1}{4}$ inch of filler.

Speaking of sanding, that process starts with the pneumatic in-line sander with 40-grit sandpaper. The goal here is to quickly smooth and level the filler. The refining stage will come later, when the pneumatic sander is traded for a handheld sanding block.

This is also where I begin to finalize the shape of the car. Remember, this is a very large, very rounded car; working on one side while viewing the opposite side is next to impossible. So how do you know when the shape is right?

GETTING THE RIGHT PROFILE

It is a rare occasion that both sides of a ride are bent and wrinkled in basically the same places in the same way. Normally, I can use one side of a vehicle as a reference guide for getting the opposite side repaired and shaped so that both sides are identical. But this car is different. Both sides of this ride have been severely modified, and those sides are very much rounded.

What's rounded got to do with it? Both sides of this ride may be rounded, but they aren't identical in shape. One may be a little more rounded than the other one, and that's exactly what I'm facing with this ride. I could easily end up with one side a little more rounded than the other side, and that's not a good thing.

USING GAUGES

To counteract that problem, I use two different profile gauges. What's a profile gauge? Much as a caliper will allow you to compare the actual condition of a part with the manufacturer's specifications for that part, a profile gauge will let you compare the actual condition, or shape, of one side of a vehicle with that of the opposite side of the same vehicle.

Both of these gauges are from Eastwood, and I start with the larger of the two (photo 4). This is the Body Panel Profile Gauge #20475, and it measures 48 inches in length. As you can see from the photo, I use this gauge to determine the actual slope of the roofline. The gauge has multiple adjustment points along its length to give a very accurate reading. Once I have the gauge set and accurately following the shape of the repair area, I move to the other side of the car and compare repairs. Any open space under any portion of the gauge indicates an area that doesn't conform to the other side of the car. The trick is in determining if the open space is a result of a low area in the plastic body filler or a high area somewhere else along the gauge, causing it to not lay flat on the surface.

Because just about every inch of the exterior of this car has a layer of plastic body filler on it, my first inclination is to mark the high spots along the length of the gauge and sand those areas using the pneumatic in-line sander to quickly cut away the excess filler. This "mark it and sand it" method works great until the yellow color of the epoxy coat begins to show through the filler; once that happens, it is time to switch from removing filler from the high spots to adding filler to the low spots.

The other gauge, Eastwood's Adjustable Profile Gauge #11192 (photo 5), is far more precise in that I can use this gauge to fine-tune just about any shape on the car. I use this gauge once I've made the switch from the pneumatic in-line sander to hand sanding blocks. Here you can see I'm using the gauge to check the roll of the roof where it meets the quarter window opening. I also use this gauge to verify the curve of the rear fenders and the shape of the lower portion of both doors.

Everything I've shown you so far has been designed to bring the shape of both sides of this car into some kind of uniformity. In body shop terms, what I've done is to rough out the car. The major metal repair problems have been taken care of, and now the car sports a very thin layer of plastic body filler that has been somewhat smoothed but is nowhere near perfect. That's next.

PHOTO 4: This Eastwood profile gauge is the perfect tool to use when comparing the slope of one side of the roof with that of the other side.

PHOTO 5: This smaller profile gauge will give you a much more refined look at the shape of a repair. Here I'm comparing the deep roll of the roof where it meets the quarter glass opening.

BLOCK SANDING

I've talked about this process before, but because it is the one step that defines the final look of any project vehicle, it is definitely worth covering again. What am I talking about? Block sanding the plastic body filler.

I covered my choice of sanding blocks in the previous chapter, so now it's time to grab some sandpaper and go to work. I start by covering the entire car with a guide coat of black paint. Try Eastwood Guide Coat #12389 Z.

A guide coat does one important thing: it highlights any imperfections in the plastic body filler so they can be repaired. What do imperfections look like? We hope most of them will look like the ones visible in photo 6. Some of these are a result of using the in-line sander, others are telltale tracks of the applicator. Neither type is serious, but blemishes like these will be plentiful all over this ride.

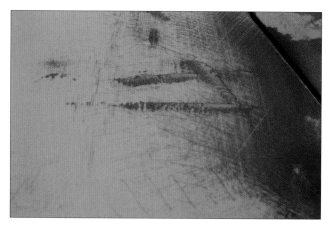

PHOTO 6: Some of these deep scratches aren't really scratches at all. They resulted from the application of the filler. Notice that each one is roughly the length of the 6-inch plastic spreader. The smaller scratches came from using the in-line sander.

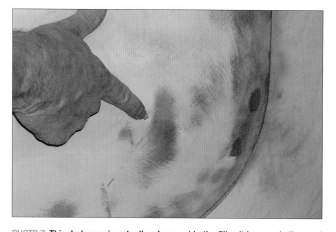

PHOTO 7: This dark area is actually a low spot in the filler. It is very shallow and probably would not have been detected without the guide coat.

But that's not the end to imperfections. Check out photo 7. What I've pointed out here is a wave in the filler that resulted in a low spot. Without the guide coat, this minute wave might never have been detected prior to painting. If you look closely, you won't see any indication of the epoxy coat showing through. That's a good sign. It means I can keep sanding using an X pattern and hopefully sand this wave smooth.

Keep sanding? Wait a minute. When did all of this sanding start? It started right after the guide coat went on and I attached a piece of 80-grit sandpaper to the 27-inch-long sanding block. Why use the 27-inch block? The longer the block, the smoother the result.

TIP

Sanding is another of those subjects covered in depth in Revive Your Ride: Secrets from a Body and Paint Restoration Pro.

Since sanding from the upper right to the lower left, then switching, is pretty monotonous, I thought I would concentrate on the problem areas that always seem to arise once the sanding starts. Let's go back to photo 6 and look at how these problems should be corrected.

PROBLEM AREAS

In a perfect world, I would keep sanding, and these problems would sand away and disappear. But one look at the depth of these scratches and mars, and it is obvious that continued sanding will not remove them. Problem areas like these are best repaired by filling them with Evercoat Metal Glaze, Eastwood #31279 Z. The one thing you don't want to do is to sand Metal Glaze with 40-grit sandpaper. A coarse sandpaper like 40 grit will literally rip the application apart and result in a complete waste of material. I prefer to sand Metal Glaze with 80-grit sandpaper. I end up with a repair that is smooth enough to prime while still coarse enough to provide good bonding for the primer to be applied later.

Now let's review photo 7. The dark area pointed out here indicates low spots in the filler. Because this repair area is rounded, I really don't want to keep sanding to try to remove the guide coat. Why not? Continued sanding in a contoured area like this will result in a flat spot.

To keep that rounded shape, this low area needs more filling capability than the Metal Glaze will provide. OK, I know what you are about to ask, so I'll answer it here. Metal Glaze should be applied only in very thin layers. How thin? Maybe $\frac{1}{16}$ inch. In this case, I may need $\frac{1}{8}$ inch thickness or more in order to retain the curve of the panel, and that can be achieved only by building up the area using Evercoat Rage body filler.

The hard part of this type of repair comes after the Rage body filler has had time to cure enough for it to be sanded. I have to sand the filler but not sand the area around it. Sound impossible? It is, but I have a technique that works great.

I start by sanding the newly applied filler with a 5-inch block. Why use such a short block? I don't want to sand anywhere other than on the applied filler. Sanding the area around the applied filler will create an over-sanded condition around the filler and an undersanded condition on the newly applied filler. The result will be a wavy surface, and that's not acceptable.

To counteract this problem, I add more guide coat and use a new sheet of sandpaper on the block. A new sheet of sandpaper will act like a sharp knife and quickly cut through the filler. The guide coat will tell me if I'm disturbing the filler surrounding the repair areas. Here is an example in photo 8. Notice that I've managed to concentrate my sanding efforts on the patch of filler and not on the surrounding filler.

But then, I'm not completely crazy. I know I'll eventually end up sanding the surrounding area. It just can't be helped. There is no way to get this small patch to blend into the surrounding repair without sanding everywhere around it. So once I have the area sanded to a point that I consider to be as smooth as possible, I complete the repair by covering the entire area with a thin coat of Metal Glaze. I then sand the Metal Glaze smooth using 80-grit sandpaper and end up with a perfectly level and smooth surface.

The only flaw in the aforementioned method is that this is a huge panel and only one of several on this car. I could use a full quart of Metal Glaze applying just a thin coat to this one panel. At $30 a quart, that step just doesn't make good economic sense. The solution is to graduate to longer blocks, a 15-inch and then a 27-inch block, depending on the size of the panel, as I sand the repaired area. After that, I switch to 100-grit sandpaper to further reduce the amount of filler being removed. I

continue with the X pattern, and as I switch to longer sanding blocks, I also expand my sanding area until I'm sanding the entire panel. The result should be a nice and smooth panel fit for priming.

How can I be sure the panel is nice and smooth? Photo 9 shows an old body man's trick you may have seen before. I use a shop towel as a buffer between my hand and the rough sanded surface of the panel. The shop towel lets my hand glide over the surface a little easier, and that in turn allows me to better feel any imperfections that might exist on the panel. Usually, those imperfections will be in the form of low spots and waves.

I hope I've made this sound easy and you're ready to try your hand at repairing your own ride. It's easy, but just for the first hour or so. After that, it becomes hard work. So with that thought in mind, let me add a few tips on the next page that I hope will alleviate some of the stress block sanding can cause.

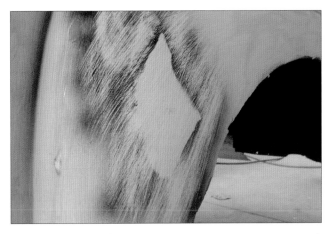

PHOTO 8: The goal here is to sand this small area of filler without overly sanding the surrounding filler. The guide coat helps me keep an eye on the process.

PHOTO 9: An old body man's trick to verify the smoothness of a panel is to use a shop towel as a buffer between your hand and the panel. Any waves, dips, or bumps can be easily felt this way.

See photo 10. Notice the arrows indicating the direction of travel for the block. This broadside attack offers the optimum sanding coverage. That equals less time spent sanding.

PHOTO 10

Photo 11 is one example of how not to sand. Think of the block as one finger of a huge hand. Like sanding a panel with your bare hands, the block held in this manner leaves long marks like finger tracks across the surface of the panel.

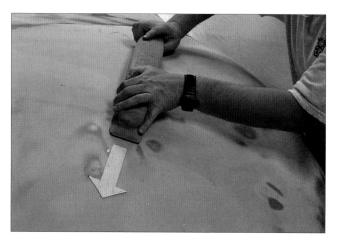

PHOTO 11

Photo 12, another example of how not to sand, should be easily understood. Moving the block straight up and down will do little more than allow it to follow any existing waves and bumps in the panel, and that will act to magnify existing problems rather than remove them.

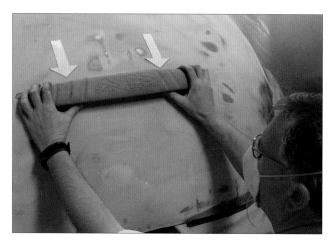

PHOTO 12

NOTES

CHAPTER 13

TIME TO
SELECT COLORS

This is going to be one of those "poke holes in the punch list" chapters, in that I am absolutely exhausted from sanding plastic body filler and need a break. Fortunately, I have a lot of things that still need to be done to this car, but they will be impacted by something else that needs to be done. I think the best next step is to look ahead to the final color scheme for this car.

I need to know what color the car is going to be painted in order to know what color the frame needs to be painted in order to know what color the engine needs to be painted in order to actually start putting finished parts back on this car for the final buildup.

THE RIGHT COLORS

When the thought of exterior colors comes to mind, you have to first think about paint manufacturer choices. For this ride, my choice of paint brands is House of Kolor (HOK). To be assured, I selected House of Kolor for its quality, but I also chose House of Kolor for its unique line of colors. I didn't want this car sporting a color that could readily be picked out from some automobile manufacturer's line of colors. I wanted this car to have a one-of-a-kind finish. So what colors did I select? Having learned at least a little something from my renowned artist mother, I know you always start with the background color and work outward. For the base color, I selected HOK #KBC10. This is a very deep purple, almost bordering on black.

Did I say colors, as in more than one? Yes, once the base purple has been applied, the '46 will be accented with a very deep red, HOK #KBC20, and a splash of Chrysler Code 7, Plum Crazy Purple. The actual paint scheme is something I have churning inside my brain at this point, and as soon as I have a little time I'll lay it out on the computer to see how it looks. But that's for later, once all of the priming and sanding has been accomplished.

PAINTING THE FRAME

One of those tasks that need to be done before something else can be done is painting the frame (photo 1). If you look closely, you can see I've stripped the frame down to the bare rails and mounted it on a new rotisserie. If you don't have a good rotisserie for painting frames, you are really missing out. This unit came from Eastwood, #12174, and is manufactured by AutoTwirler, one of the top names in rotisserie units. I hate to admit it, but in the past I have often reinvented the wheel, so to speak, when it came to

PHOTO 1: The frame has been stripped down to the bare rails and mounted on a new rotisserie manufactured by AutoTwirler.

rotisseries. I've built them, bought them, custom ordered them, and done without them. I've used them, abused them, sold them, and given them away. Having put this unit through its paces with great success, I'm thinking it is going to be a keeper.

It is built strong, uses hydraulics to help raise and lower whatever is mounted on the unit, has a great fine-tune adjustment feature that ensures that whatever is mounted on the unit can be perfectly balanced to make rotation a snap—and it is user friendly enough that only minutes are required to position and mount whatever needs mounting. I'll give you more information on this unit, in particular what it takes to mount something so that it is properly balanced, once I'm ready to mount the body of the '46 and flip it over for some underneath repair and painting.

APPLYING A LITTLE RED PAINT

Back when this project first began, I thoroughly sanded the frame using 320-grit sandpaper. After that, I gave it a coat of Eastwood Rust Encapsulator #16065ZP to keep rust at bay while I made the needed structural modifications. All of that took place some time ago, and now I'm ready to make this frame beautiful.

The plan calls for giving this vehicle a very eye-popping appearance anytime someone looks under the car or inside the engine compartment. To do that, I decided the frame needs to be painted a very deep red. Contrasted against the deep purple background of the body, the underside of this ride will pop. I'll add to the red look of the frame by also painting the engine red, then adding a few chrome goodies to make the power plant sparkle. I may need sunglasses just to open the hood.

But before I can spray any red paint on this frame, I need to smooth out the welds and joints by filling them with a thin layer of Evercoat Rage body filler. The purpose of this exercise is to make the frame look cosmetically finished.

PREP

I start once again by sanding the frame to prep it for priming. This time, I use 180-grit sandpaper. The coat of Rust Encapsulator already on the frame will accept plastic body filler, but it must be sanded in order to provide a good bond. After that, the filler can be applied and sanded smooth.

Check out photo 2. You'll notice that everywhere I made a modification to the frame, I smoothed that modification by adding a layer of Evercoat Rage body filler. I use 80-grit sandpaper to smooth the filler once it has cured. It takes more time than sanding with 40-grit, but the reduction in sand scratches that will have to be sanded out once the primer is applied will more than make up for the time lost sanding with 80 grit. Also notice that I masked off portions of the new rotisserie. I'll be priming the frame soon, and I'd rather not have overspray settling on the machine. I like a clean machine.

Since I'm going to be using House of Kolor paints, I'll also use House of Kolor primers and sealers to refinish the frame. The primer/surfacer of choice is HOK #KP-2CF Chromate Free Epoxy Primer surfacer. This is a two-part product that mixes one part A to one part B and will be sprayed using the Binks M1-G HVLP (Eastwood #34160) with a 1.4 mm spray tip. I apply two coats.

Once the primer has cured, usually overnight, I sand it smooth using 320-grit sandpaper and finish with a single coat of House of Kolor #KS10 sealer. This is a white seal coat that mixes at 4:1:1, four parts sealer to one part #KU150 hardener to one part #RU310 reducer. The RU 310 reducer is a fast-drying reducer, exactly what I need to prevent runs in and around all of the intricate, detailed areas of the frame. Application is made using another Binks M1-G HVLP with a smaller, 1.3 mm spray tip.

Why the smaller spray tip? It is a matter of atomization. The thicker primer needs a larger spray tip to provide proper atomization to lay down nice and smooth. The thinner seal coat sprays and atomizes better with the smaller tip, and the result is an even smoother finish.

PHOTO 2: Every weld point is being smoothed by adding a thin coat of Rage body filler. The result will be a very smooth and finished frame.

The red base color, HOK #KBC20 is also mixed 1:1, one part base color to one part RU310 reducer. Again, I use the fast-drying reducer to hurry up the drying process and prevent any runs. I apply three medium-wet coats using the Binks M1-G HVLP spray gun with a 1.3 mm spray tip.

The clear coat, HOK #UC35, is mixed 2:1:1, two parts UC35 clear to one part KU150 hardener to one part RU310 reducer. I apply three medium-wet coats using the DeVilbiss GFG-670 Plus gravity feed spray gun (Eastwood #34227) with a 1.3 mm spray tip. What was the result of all this work? Check out photo 3.

OK, I can hear what you are thinking: three different paint guns? Yes. The luxury of three spray guns allows me to dedicate a particular spray gun to a particular task. For example, the Binks M1-G HVLP with the 1.4 mm spray tip is used to spray primer only. The Binks M1-G HVLP with the 1.3 mm spray tip is used to spray seal coats and base color coats only. The DeVilbiss GFG-670 Plus sprays nothing but clear coats.

Why dedicate the spray guns? Here's an extreme case. I spray a base color through the same spray gun I use to spray clear coats and fail to remove all traces of the base color from the gun before loading it with clear. I begin spraying clear and suddenly out comes a lump of

PHOTO 3: The finished frame. It's bright! It's going to look good once all the parts are on it.

red, or some other color, on the clear coat I just sprayed over a white base. That's a problem I don't need, and the best way to prevent that problem is to never spray colors through the same paint gun I use to spray clear coats.

PAINTING THE ENGINE

I often hear people complain that all their hard work painting an engine was for naught because the paint flaked off. They think the problem is the paint's failure to withstand the heat of the engine. That's rarely the case. A very hot engine will run around 220 to 240 degrees F. That's not enough heat to peel most paints. If the paint is flaking off, it is most likely due to the failure to properly prepare the engine for paint, not the failure of the paint.

Consider how many people didn't know their vintage Chevrolet 350 engine was painted bright orange until it was removed from a greasy engine bay and washed. That paint stayed on, and it was sprayed from lowly enamel stock. So why can't people get the paint to stay on their engines? They fail to properly clean and degrease the engine.

CLEANING THE ENGINE

How do you clean an engine? Time was I brought out the pressure washer to blast away the grease and grime, then sanded and sanded until every inch of the engine was clean. Today, I rarely do that. Instead, I follow one of two different courses.

In the event the engine is destined for a rebuild, which will be the case for the Chevy 350 going into this ride, I let the machine shop soak the engine components in a cleaning vat that removes everything but the casting numbers. I leave explicit instructions that they are not to paint anything once the machining has been completed. Once I have the engine back in my shop—by the way, I never let my machinist do the actual rebuild—I assemble the components and give the rebuilt unit a thorough degreasing and sanding before painting. Why do I assemble my own engines? I enjoy the process.

In the case where the engine is not to be rebuilt, such as when purchasing a crate motor, I tape off all of the openings with duct tape—that's "two hundred mile an hour tape" for you NASCAR fans—and have the assembled unit soda blasted clean. After that, a little degreasing with PPG DX 330 degreaser and the unit is ready for paint.

How do I refinish an engine? That starts with another thorough cleaning with a mild dish washing detergent soap, such as Dawn, and degreasing using PPG DX 330 degreaser. After that, I give the engine two coats of epoxy. My preference is PPG DP40LF mixed 2:1 with DP 402LF Catalyst and sprayed through the Binks M1-G HVLP spray gun with the 1.4 mm spray tip. After one hour cure time, I complete the process by adding three coats of HOK #KBC20 red and three coats of HOK #UC35 clear coat.

What am I doing mixing paint brands? Normally I would not, but the PPG DP40LF epoxy sprays on extremely smooth, and that translates into not having to sand the engine before the color coats are applied. Photo 4 shows the end result.

LET THE FRAME ASSEMBLY WORK BEGIN

If you recall, I did a little head scratching trying to decide how best to handle the fuel tank situation in this car. Fortunately, the solution to the problem had been taking

PHOTO 4: The engine after painting and assembly.

PHOTO 5: The fuel tank gets a thorough cleaning and a fresh paint job.

up space in the storage building all along. All I had to do was retrieve it, fit it to the frame, then send it out to be cleaned and leak checked. Where did the tank come from? Originally, the tank was mounted under an early model Mustang. The side mounting flanges and rear mounted fuel inlet made this the perfect tank for the '46 Ford.

To ensure that the tank would be completely trouble free, I turned to Eastwood for its Gas Tank Sealer Kit #10165 Z and a couple of cans of Tank Tone Metallic Coating #10030 Z. The Gas Tank Sealer Kit ensures that any rust or small leak problems will not develop inside the tank, and the Tank Tone Metallic Coating will give this old tank a new look (photo 5).

That brings me to selecting the gauges for this car, because I need to be sure the fuel tank sending unit is correctly calibrated to the fuel gauge. I don't want the fuel gauge telling me the tank is half full while I'm pushing the car to the nearest gas station.

The gauges I selected are from Auto Meter and include a speedometer, tachometer, oil pressure gauge, temperature gauge, volt gauge, fuel gauge, and clock. (photo 6). These are nostalgic-style gauges, as opposed to the latest trend of digital readouts, and I think they will look and work great in this car.

The Auto Meter gauge kit comes with a complete set of installation instructions to be sure everything is wired correctly. One of those instructions includes information on the required ohm values of the fuel tank sending unit. In this case, I'll be using a Ford sending unit with a 12–15 ohm value when the gauge reads full, and a 75 ohm value when the gauge reads empty.

Having carefully read the fuel gauge instructions that came with the Auto Meter gauges, I know the

PHOTO 6: The set of nostalgic-style new gauges from Auto Meter.

gauge is compatible with my sending unit and will read empty when the tank is dry and full when I have enough money to fill it up.

INSTALLING THE REAR AXLE ASSEMBLY

I've had this unit mounted in the frame for some time now, so all I need to do is remove it, paint it, and install it for a final time. I'll paint the axle unit and the four mounting arms red to match the frame, then offset the red look by adding chrome coil-over shocks (photo 7).

INSTALLING THE FRONT SUSPENSION

Moving forward, much of the front suspension will receive the same red finish I gave the frame and rear axle assembly. But because the front suspension is a point of the car that is often scrutinized by curious enthusiasts, I decide to try a new powder coating product from Eastwood that promises a look close to actual chrome.

I painted some of the parts red and used the Eastwood Elite HotCoat Kit #12859 and Hotcoat Single Stage Reflective Chrome Powder #11504 to finish the other pieces. Photo 8 shows the result. It isn't quite chrome, but it isn't far from it either.

Of course, there are a few tidbits of information you should know before attempting to powder coat any metal parts. To start with, any part being powder coated must be cleaned down to the bare metal. I use the Eastwood #22107 blast cabinet with #22021 aluminum oxide blast media to remove all traces of old paint, rust, and grease. After that, the parts must be baked in an electric oven at 350 degrees F for about thirty minutes to leach out any remaining grease residue. Then, the parts are degreased with PPG DX 330 and the powder coat applied using the HotCoat kit. Finally, the parts are baked in the electric oven for thirty to forty-five minutes at 400 degrees F.

> ### TIP
>
> *Coil springs are the exception to the thirty to forty-five minutes at 400 degrees rule. They must never be heated above 325 degrees F. To do so could remove some of the temper from the springs and reduce their effectiveness.*

That brings me to the last item on the punch list, installing the front suspension pieces. I start by mounting both the upper and lower control arms and the spindles. Notice that I left the springs out of the suspension (photo 9). They will go in later. Next, the lower control arm is leveled using a small carpenter's level. Now I can attach the magnetic protractor to the face of the spindle and set the upper control arm so that the protractor is reading zero. That ensures that the spindle is straight up and down, which equals zero caster on the front-end alignment setting. I'm not concerned with the camber setting as it is best made by a professional using state-of-the-art front-end alignment equipment once the car has been finished. All I'm looking for here is an initial setup that will let me build up the car.

PHOTO 7: The rear axle assembly is also painted bright red before being installed on the car.

PHOTO 8: Some of these front suspension pieces were painted red, the rest were powder coated with Single Stage Reflective Chrome Powder. I like the results.

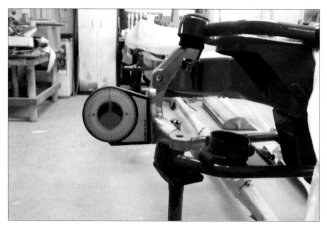

PHOTO 9: The control arms and spindle are installed minus the spring. It will go in later.

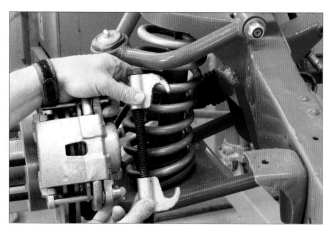

PHOTO 10: I used this Eastwood Coilspring Compressor to compress the springs for installation. This is the safest way to mount any suspension spring.

Last, the springs can go in. To install the springs, I use the Eastwood Coilspring Compressor #49031 to compress each spring before loosening the lower control arm to allow installation (photo 10).

So how does the frame look with most of the goodies installed? I'm still waiting for the transmission to return before I can bolt in the engine, but everything else is looking good (photo 11).

Notice that I used the AutoTwirler rotisserie as a building platform to assemble the frame. It's nice to be able to place a frame at a comfortable working height, and this rotisserie allowed me to do just that.

PHOTO 11: The completed frame.

NOTES

CHAPTER 14

NEW PARTS
AND FRESH PRIMER

'm happy to report that after 5 gallons of Evercoat Rage body filler, I've reached my goal of perfecting the body of the '46. Did I say 5 gallons? Yes, I did. But let me qualify the need for so much body filler. This is a huge car, and every inch of it needed at least one coat of filler. It took 3 gallons just to go around the car one time. I'm talking repairing all of the exterior panels plus the fenders, hood, deck lid, doors and door jambs, and the firewall. Yep, I'm exhausted.

PRIMING THE CAR

But knowing I've reached this milestone is enough to reenergize me and send me to the mixing bench for a little primer/surfacer. The primer of choice is House of Kolor #KP-2CF Chromate Free Epoxy Primer parts A and B. This is the same product I used previously to apply the initial epoxy coat to the bare sheet metal skins of this car and to prime the frame for painting. I mix the primer 1:1, 1 part A to 1 part B, and apply the primer using the Binks M1-G with a 1.4 mm spray tip. The body gets three medium-wet coats (photo 1).

Once the primer has cured, it gets covered with a thin black guide coat to make locating all of the imperfections a little easier as I sand the primer smooth. What's the guide coat? In this case, I'm using Eastwood Guide Coat #12389 Z.

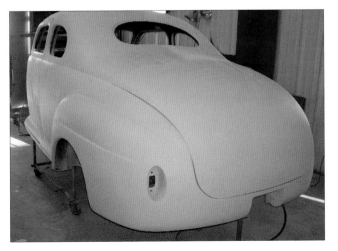

PHOTO 1: Three coats of HOK primer have drastically improved the looks of this car.

But what I'm not going to do at this time is begin the block sanding process. Why not? I've barely had time to recover from sanding the plastic body filler. That's one reason. Another reason is that I want to mount the body on the AutoTwirler rotisserie and complete some repairs to the underside. The last reason is that I only primed the car at this point to prevent the exposed areas of bare metal from developing surface rust. If not for those reasons, I would completely ignore all of that plastic body filler, at least for a while.

MOUNTING THE BODY ON THE AUTOTWIRLER ROTISSERIE

When it comes to correctly mounting anything on a rotisserie, balance is the key. Let's say you mount the body of your ride on a rotisserie using the mounting points where the body attaches to the frame. If you stand back and look at the way the car is mounted, it might lead you to believe the body will be top heavy and, once the safety locks on the rotisserie are loosened, it will do a 180-degree flip and hang there until you gather enough beer-drinking buddies to muscle it back around to a comfortable working position.

Luckily, that's just not the case. Even though most car bodies look top heavy, the bulk of the weight is actually located along a line just above the floor pan.

So are the body-to-frame mounting points the best places to attach a body to a rotisserie? In most cases, yes. This is about as close to finding and using the imaginary centerline of balance within the body as there is. The body may still be a little top heavy, but not enough to cause a problem when turning it on the rotisserie.

To mount the body on the AutoTwirler rotisserie, I start by lowering the hydraulic rams to their lowest points, then use the fine-tune adjustment screws to position the mounting beams to the correct height for attaching the beams to the car. How does that work?

Each end of this rotisserie has two separate lifting points, one that the hydraulic ram controls and another that is controlled by the fine-tune adjustment screw located just above the rotisserie pivot tube. Photo 2 is a close-up shot of one of the fine-tune adjustment screws. Referring to photo 4, you can see where adjusting this screw will cause the mounting beam on the pivot tube to move either up or down independent of the main lifting beam, which is controlled by the hydraulic ram.

Photo 3 shows the right-hand front mounting point for the rotisserie. This is also where the body mounts to the frame. Located a few inches below the centerline of the car and just above the forward bottom of the rocker panel, this is also one of the stronger points of the body. I use 3-inch-long ⅜-inch bolts to attach the rotisserie mounting arms to both sides of the body.

Photo 4 shows the rear mounting points for the rotisserie. Back here my mounting point choices are limited. I need a structurally strong area, but one that would be easily accessible to the rotisserie. I also need mounting points located at or above the aforementioned centerline of the car to help offset having used mounting points at the front of the car that were below the centerline. The rear body-to-frame mounting points prove to be just about perfect when accessed from inside the trunk compartment. As I did with the front mounts, I use 3-inch-long ⅜-inch bolts to secure the rotisserie mounting arms to the car.

FINE-TUNING THE BALANCE

The next step is to place both mounting beams at the same height. Why do both mounting beams have to be at the same height? We're back to that balance thing being the key again. I need to be sure both end units are on the same turning axis, or whatever is mounted on the unit simply will not turn. Something will have to give, and more than likely, considering the strength of the AutoTwirler unit, what will give will be the mounting points on the body. Having both ends of the rotis-

PHOTO 2: A close-up view of the fine-tune adjustment screw used to move the mounting beam on the pivot tube up or down.

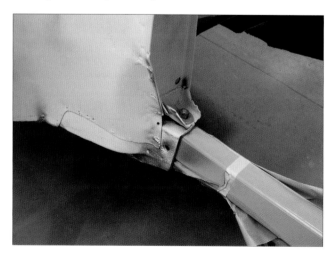

PHOTO 3: A close-up of the right-hand front mounting point for the rotisserie. This is also the forward mounting point for bolting the body to the frame.

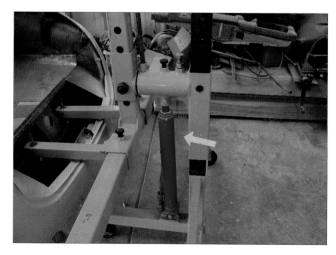

PHOTO 4: At the rear of the car, I've reached the rotisserie mounting bars inside the trunk compartment to access the rear body-to-frame mounting points.

serie on the same turning axis allows me to easily turn the body of the '46.

I've already measured the distance from the mounting beam to the floor at the front of the car and have locked down the beam at 41 inches using the built-in locking bolts on the rotisserie. I verify that measurement at the back of the body by setting the rear mounting beam as close to 41 inches from the floor as possible (photo 5).

This brings me back to having placed the hydraulic rams at their lowest points. I can now raise the car body as much as is needed to roll the body completely over, or lower the body as much as is needed to readily access any part of the body to do repairs comfortably. The only trick here is to always raise or lower the hydraulic rams equally to ensure the turning axis of each end stays at the same height. One of the reasons for taking the time to set both mounting beams at the same height is that it lets me use the locking bolts as guides to be sure I raise or lower the hydraulic rams equally.

How long did it take to mount the body on the AutoTwirler rotisserie? This is such a well-designed and well-thought-out unit that I spent a whopping fifteen minutes mounting the body of the '46.

PAINTING THE UNDERSIDE

The repairs to the underside are minor, consisting of little more than the need to finish up some welds along the sides of the new floor pans and to add an additional cross brace under the trunk floor pan just forward of the fuel tank inlet access opening. I want a little extra support back here should the trophies I'll be gathering start to get a little heavy. With that out of the way, I can concentrate on putting a final finish under here.

I made the decision some time ago to give the underside of the body a textured finish. I'll still be painting the underside the same deep purple as the exterior, but I don't want a hard, slick finish that could easily be chipped as this ride rolls down the road to the next car show. So now I'm in search of a product that will not only give me the tough, textured finish I desire but also one that can be painted. That leads me to the LizardSkin line.

For the underside of the car, I select LizardSkin Ceramic Insulation (photo 6). This product decreases engine and solar heat transfer anywhere from 25 to 30 percent, reduces road noise up to 12 decibels, resists moisture penetration, and can withstand exhaust temperatures up to 500 degrees F. I'm not sure what else you could ask of an insulating product.

This is a spray-on application, and it goes on at roughly 15 mils per coat. The recommended application is three coats for a total coverage thickness of about 45 mils. You can expect to get 20–25 square feet of coverage per gallon. I use 2 gallons to coat the underside of the '46. I purchased an extra gallon to cover things like the front fenders and fender skirts, which I'll be working on later.

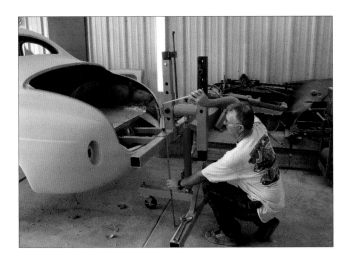

PHOTO 5: Here I'm measuring the height of the mounting beam. I'll set the height of the front mounting beam at the same height.

PHOTO 6: LizardSkin Ceramic Insulation. This is one of the best insulating and undercoating products I've used.

As you can see in photo 7, even though the application is textured, the product is heavy enough to fill most imperfections for a very uniform finish.

But I don't stop there. I also want something to insulate and seal up the inside of the car. For that, I choose LizardSkin Sound Control (SC) Formula (photo 8). The stated intended use for this product is to vastly improve upon the sound quality emanating from the eight-track player. It also improves the sounds from the latest digital creations, if you happen to understand how those things work.

The LizardSkin SC product is also a spray-on application, and it will cover roughly 50 square feet when it is applied at 15 mils per coat with a two-coat application (photo 9).

I allow the LizardSkin products to cure for forty-eight hours, then go back and finish the underside of the car

with three coats of HOK #KBC10 purple and two coats of HOK #UC35 clear (photo 10).

Can I tell any difference in the car after the application? Yes, I can. When working on the body, the car no longer bangs around like a tin can. Now it has a very solid, very thick sound to it. Climbing inside the car now is like throwing a blanket over your head, not at all like before, which was like climbing into an empty metal bucket.

STARTING THE BLOCK SANDING PROCESS

Did I forget to mention earlier that one of the reasons I primed the outside of the body and then left it alone was to allow my brain a little time to shift from the sanding body filler mode to the sanding primer mode? No? Well, on the outside, these appear to be two very similar processes, but when it comes time to switch from 80 grit to 320 grit, the world changes, and an entirely new mind-set becomes necessary.

But before I go down that road, let me offer a little more explanation of the priming process. As already mentioned, this car will ultimately be painted a very deep purple; it will have other colors as accents, but most of the car will be deep purple. In some lighting, the car will appear to be black. Because dark colors tend to show any and all imperfections, painting a car a dark color requires something of a different approach when it comes to priming and final sanding. That approach calls for using 120-grit sandpaper for the first sanding, then applying more guide

PHOTO 7: The underside of the '46 with a heavy coating of LizardSkin Ceramic Insulation.

PHOTO 8: LizardSkin Sound Control (SC) Formula. This product is designed for use inside a vehicle. I'll use it to coat every inch of the interior and trunk compartment.

PHOTO 9: The SC Formula sprays on easily and helps give the car a very solid look and feel.

PHOTO 10: The last step is to refinish the underside of the body with a coat of HOK #KBC10 purple, and cover that with a coat of UC35 polyurethane clear.

PHOTO 11: The initial coat of primer is on the car and a guide coat has been applied. The body is ready for sanding.

coat, followed by another sanding using 220-grit sandpaper. Won't that remove most of the primer? Yes, it will. But at this point, I'm not concerned with the loss of primer. I'm looking for imperfections, and the best way to find them is to start sanding and let the guide coat applied earlier (photo 11) show me where they are located.

Once I find all of the remaining imperfections, I use Evercoat Metal Glaze, Eastwood #31279 Z, to fill the problem areas, and then I sand that smooth using 120-grit sandpaper (photo 12).

But then, as I've mentioned, there is a different mind-set when sanding primer as opposed to sanding plastic body filler. Consider that sanding plastic body filler calls for very coarse sandpapers used with enough physical pressure to literally gouge out and remove the excess filler from a repair area. Whether you realize it or not, your mind has already determined how the repaired panel must look and feel as you go about removing the excess filler. Once you reach that point, the point where your mind tells you to stop sanding, the repair should be about as smooth as it is going to get. You're sweating, your arms ache, and the air is filled with sanding dust.

Sanding primer, on the other hand, calls for finer sandpapers used with just enough physical pressure to carefully sand only partially through a layer of soft primer. Your mind is beginning to digest the idea of sanding just enough to remove a guide coat but not so much as to expose the filler beneath. You just went from shaping and forming to smoothing and leveling, two very different processes.

PHOTO 12: Several areas require a thin coat of Metal Glaze for filling. Most of these spots are deep sand scratches, but one or two are actual low spots.

As you look at the photographs, particularly photo 12, it appears that I did more than just remove the guide coat. That's right, I did, but let me explain. I started sanding using 120 grit and graduated down to 220 grit. Those are pretty coarse sandpapers to be using on a coat of primer. This technique removes most of the primer, but that's all right. My intent was to locate imperfections and bring the surface down to the smoothness 220-grit sandpaper gives it. Obviously, I made several small repairs and filled numerous sand scratches using Metal Glaze as I worked, but then that was my goal: to bring the surface closer to perfection.

So what's next? More primer. I'll add another three coats of primer and start the sanding process all over again. Only this time, I'll start with 320-grit sandpaper and graduate down to 400-grit sandpaper. The result should be a body that is smoother than the idle on a '59 Mercury.

NOTES

NOTES

CHAPTER 15

ORDERING
CRITICAL PARTS

You might think I would be ready to talk exterior painting. After all, the car has been primed and block sanded, so it should be ready for paint. Well it is, and I would like nothing better than to mix a little color and turn this ride into a dark, shiny machine. However, I can't, or more to the point, won't. Not just yet. To do so would keep me from completing this project on schedule. To prevent that from happening, I need to look past the final coat of clear to be applied to this car and think about all of those critical parts that need to be ordered for delivery the day after the paint dries. For instance, how is this car going to be wired? Will the wires run along the frame rails or be routed somewhere inside the car? Do I have the wiring needed to accomplish such a task?

I'll be adding multi-port fuel injection (MPFI) to the engine to bring this ride up to modern standards as far as fuel management is concerned. Is there any part of a MPFI kit that will require additional modifications to the frame, which are best done before the body is mounted?

Then there is the glass situation. It can take weeks to have glass custom cut and fit to a ride. With the chopped top on this car, standard-size glass is out of the question. I'll need to call my glass guy and get on his list. As soon as the body has been painted, I'll be in need of some glass.

Last, there is the interior trim. I'll be doing most of that work myself, but I'll still need to decide on the colors and place an order for some vinyl and carpet.

These are all concerns that need to be addressed now, while the purple paint is on the shaker and the spray guns are still on the bench. I'll start by addressing the first question about wiring this ride.

TIP

Making a list of the things that need to be done then checking off each one as you move through them helps you keep on top of all those little things that can often be overlooked on a project of this size.

WIRING

Without a doubt, Painless Performance Products is my first choice of providers when it comes to wiring anything. Painless has a wiring package designed to handle just about anything on the road. It also carries all of the nitpicky things you don't realize you need until you recognize something is missing or that something not quite so "salvage yard" would look much better. You can browse the Eastwood Web site for Painless Performance Products or go straight to the Painless Performance Products Web site. Either way, the best results are obtained first by reviewing all of the options and accessories Painless has to offer, then by compiling a list of those things that will be needed to correctly wire the project at hand. For example, will the car be using an electric fuel pump? In this case, an electric fuel pump will be needed for the MPFI unit. Is an additional harness needed to wire the pump? Will salvage yard switches be used to handle operations like illuminating the headlights and turning on the windshield wipers? Will those switches look appropriate to the car, or would custom switches look better? What about the steering column? Will it require a GM wiring connector or will it need something custom made? These are just a few questions taken from a long list of questions that will need to be addressed in order to properly wire a car.

Photo 1 shows my selections for the '46. I opted for the Painless Performance 18 Circuit Universal Streetrod Harness #10202, the 6-Pack Relay Bank #30108 (this harness is great for vehicles with power windows), Master Disconnect Switch with Panel #50710 (to shut down the electrical system for winter storage), Fuel Pump Relay Kit #50102 (for the fuel injection system), Fan Relay #30129 (for use with the electric cooling fan), Headlight Switch #80152, Windshield Wiper Switch #80173, Brake Light Switch #80172, and three sizes of Split Braided Sleeving: ¼-inch, #70901; ½-inch, #70902; ¾-inch, #70903. The split braided sleeves shroud the wires and give the overall wiring a very professional look.

I also made the decision to route the main wiring harness throughout the inside of the car so no additional work to the frame will be required to get voltage to the rear of the car, where I'll have lights and an electrically operated flip-down rear license plate pocket.

FUEL INJECTION

As for the MPFI unit, I elected to go with Affordable Fuel Injection. If you prefer Throttle Body Injection (TBI), Affordable can do that also. I went with the MPFI system because the high-rise polished aluminum intake manifold Affordable uses with its system looks totally retro, and it will be in keeping with a more traditional hot rod look (photo 2).

After reading the instruction manual that comes with the MPFI kit—and, by the way, the manual is very well

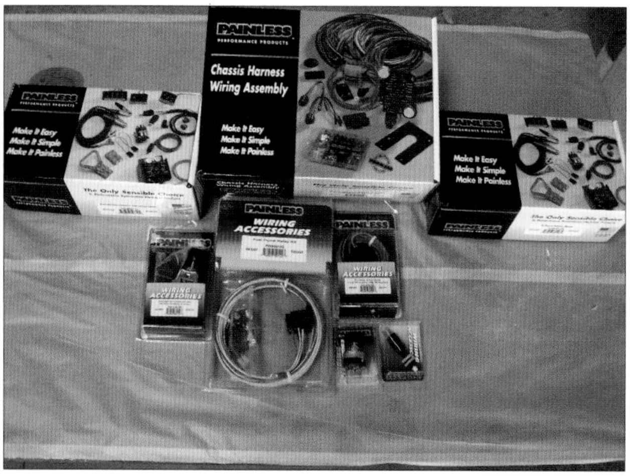

PHOTO 1: Painless Performance Products has everything needed to properly wire the '46. Here are the basic components.

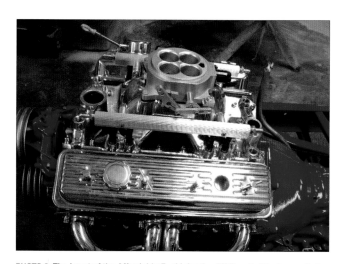

PHOTO 2: The heart of the Affordable Fuel Injection MPFI unit. It looks great atop the engine in the '46.

written and easy to follow—I determined I'll need to route a fuel return line from the engine back to the fuel tank. This line will be made of $\frac{5}{16}$-inch steel tubing, and I'll route it alongside the previously routed fuel delivery line mounted inside the left frame rail.

Since the fuel tank I'm using doesn't have provisions for a fuel return line, I'll incorporate an inlet in the filler neck so that there will be no need to remove the tank from the frame and have an inlet welded to the top of the tank. That would be a "professional only" task, something I wouldn't attempt here in the shop.

GLASS

Last on the list is the glass. The windshield, both door glasses, and both quarter windows will need to be cut to size. The back glass opening was left original, so all I need to do there is purchase a replacement glass for that opening.

A few months ago, I asked my glass guy to drop by the shop to discuss the possible ways we could get new glass into the car. This is some more of that preplanning stuff that makes a huge project like this flow a little more smoothly. Our decision was to urethane set the windshield and two quarter glasses and finish them on the outside with a thin black plastic bead situated between the glass and the surrounding metal. The black plastic bead will be a product similar to the material GM used in the '80s to set windshields in their vehicles.

The door glasses will also need to be specially cut, which leads me to the subject of templates. I don't want my glass guy spending his expensive time cutting and fitting a template for the door glasses. This is something I can do myself and save a few bucks in the process. All I need to do is cut a cardboard template to fit the opening, then transfer that template to a sheet of Masonite, and then cut a slightly larger version from the Masonite. Why larger? I can trim the piece down to size, but I can't water the Masonite and expect it to grow to fit. I can do the same thing for the quarter glasses, as all they need to do is sit in an opening where they will butt against the metal surround. No need for critical sizing and fitting here.

The windshield opening is a different matter. Here I need the glass cut large enough to overlap the original metal opening so that it doesn't fall though the hole, yet it still needs to be small enough to accept the plastic bead

that will be used to go around the glass. This is why you call a glass guy. He's been there, done that before, and he will be the one cutting and fitting the windshield.

So with those details out of the way, now it is time to pry open a can or two of paint.

PAINT

The HOK #KBC10 purple base coat comes in quart cans. I have a total of 8 quarts, and the first thing I need to do is combine all 8 quarts to be sure the color is consistent from the first part sprayed to the last part sprayed. To mix the color, I paid a visit to my local home improvement center and purchased a 2-gallon plastic bucket and two 1-gallon paint cans. I poured all 8 quarts of color into the plastic bucket, stirred thoroughly, then divided the mix equally between the two 1-gallon paint cans.

From this point forward, you may think the method I'm going to use to paint this car is a bit unorthodox. In some shops it may be, but for me this is the best way to proceed. I'll be working alone, and once I begin mixing and spraying colors, the clock starts ticking. I have only a short window of twelve hours between spraying the first color coat and the need to lock that color down with a coat of clear, or I have to stop, sand the car, and start over.

Sometime during that twelve-hour window, between spraying the base purple color and spraying the clear coats, I have two additional colors to apply to the car. Each color needs at least an hour of cure time before it can be taped over so the next color can be applied. That's more than half a day gone just spraying the additional colors, and I have yet to factor in the layout of a color scheme tape line for each of those colors, which when finished on one side of the car will have to be duplicated on the other side of the car. For that, you can estimate one to two hours per color. That's another six to eight hours minimum if all goes well, and I will still have at least four coats of clear needing an additional two to three hours to apply on top of that. That adds up to one long, long day.

But that's not all. In addition to spending hours behind a spray gun, I also need to remove the body from the rotisserie and mount it on the frame, install the doors, lay out and paint the graphic colors on the doors, remove the doors so they can be clear coated separately, install the deck lid, lay out and paint the graphic colors that extend onto the deck lid, and then remove it so it can be clear coated separately.

What's the deal with removing the doors and deck lid to clear coat them? Actually, it's to facilitate easy access to the body openings around these components. Once they are off the car, it will be very easy to clear coat them on the bench.

STIRRING SOME PAINT

Something I learned a long time ago is that good help can be expected to perform at peak efficiency for about eight hours. After ten hours the efficiency begins to drop, and after fourteen hours mistakes begin to happen. Paint costs on average around $75.00 per ready-to-spray quart for the colors I'm using, and polyurethane clear coat products average around $300.00 per ready-to-spray gallon. At these rates, any mistake can be very costly.

To prevent costly mistakes, my plan calls for breaking the painting process into two separate parts. To start, I'll apply the seal coat, the black under base coats, and purple base color coats to the body only. That will take most of the day. Once the purple dries for an hour, I'll cover the sides of the car with a single coat of clear, the roof with two coats, and the firewall with three coats.

Why a single coat of clear to the sides of the car, two coats to the roof, and three coats on the firewall? In case you forgot, the body of the '46 is still on the rotisserie. It will save me a lot of physical grief trying to reach the hard-to-get-at places such as the roof, when all I have to do now is turn the body and the roof is right there and easy to paint. That's a big

TIP

Looking for a good portable work bench for painting parts? Try the Eastwood Work Stand #43120.

thing when you have a seal coat, three under base coats, and three base color coats to apply to the roof before the clear coats can be applied. All I will need to do later, once all of the colors are on the car, is apply my additional coats of clear to complete the painting process. That I can easily manage once the body is back on the frame.

As for giving the firewall three coats of clear, that will complete this part of the car, and I won't have to contend with trying to paint around the engine and transmission after the body is back on the frame (photo 3). I'll mask off the firewall to keep overspray off of it as I continue the painting process.

That is what it will take just to get the purple on the car; I still have the graphic colors to contend with. Which brings me back to the need to mount the body back on the frame.

I can't lay out the graphic colors correctly without having the doors and deck lid back on the car. Yes, both doors and the deck lid will have to be painted purple and locked down with a coat of clear prior to being installed back on the car for the graphic color work. That will allow me to start on the graphic work in the morning and have it done by the end of the day. I can then cover the graphic colors with a coat of clear and come back the next day and lightly sand that area using 1000-grit sandpaper before completing the painting process with additional coats of clear.

The sequence of events will unfold like this. First, I apply a single, medium-wet coat of sealer to the body. The sealer of choice is HOK #KS10. This is a white seal coat that mixes 2:1:1, two parts sealer to one part KU150 hardener to one part RU310 reducer. I apply the single coat using the Binks M1-G with a 1.3 mm spray tip (photo 4).

The sealer needs an hour to cure before I can apply the black under base, over which I apply three coats of HOK #KBC10 purple. The black is HOK #BC25 Base and is needed

PHOTO 3: The completed firewall. This is going to be one nice-looking ride.

PHOTO 4: The white seal coat is applied first.

PHOTO 5: The black under base is applied next.

because the purple is a very transparent color. Without the black base, I would need to apply from eight to ten coats of KBC10 purple to obtain good coverage. By applying three coats of black under base, I can reduce the number of coats of KBC10 purple down to three. That saves me time and money.

HOK #BC25 is mixed 2:1 with RU310 reducer and applied medium-wet using the Binks M1-G with a 1.3 mm spray tip (photo 5).

HOK #KBC10 purple is also mixed 2:1 with RU310 reducer and applied medium-wet using the same Binks M1-G (photo 6).

The clear coat is HOK #UC35 polyurethane clear and is mixed 2:1:1, two parts clear to one part KU150 hardener to one part RU310 reducer. These coats are applied medium-wet using a DeVilbiss GFG-670 Plus gravity feed spray gun with a 1.3 mm spray tip (photo 7).

PHOTO 6: The purple base color goes on next.

PAINTING THE DOORS AND DECK LID

Next on my list for painting are the doors and deck lid. I'll give them the same treatment I gave the body, starting with the doors. I'll apply a seal coat, three coats of black under base, three coats of purple base color, and a single coat of clear on both the inside and the outside. I may elect to continue the graphic work inside the door frames, thus the need for only one coat of clear. The outside of the trunk will also receive a single coat of clear, but the inside of the trunk will be finished with three coats of clear. No graphic work inside there.

I'm going to give all of these parts of the car at least twenty-four hours to cure, after which I'll lightly wet sand everything but the inside of the trunk using 1000-grit sandpaper. That preps everything for the graphic colors to be applied next. What's the deal with the inside of the trunk? It will be upholstered, so no additional painting is required.

You will notice that I didn't mention painting the hood and front fenders. The front fenders will be painted purple, so I can paint them whenever I have the time and simply bolt them on. They don't present a problem. The hood, however, is a different story. The color scheme layout for the sides of the car actually begins near the front edge of the hood and

PHOTO 7: The coat of clear is next. My, what a difference a little clear can make!

moves back along the sides of the car. What that means is that the hood must be in perfect alignment with the body in order to ensure that the graphic lines stay straight. I can't do that until the front sheet metal has been installed, and I can't install the front sheet metal until the body has been painted.

THE GRAPHICS

The trick to being sure I have the graphic lines straight without the hood being mounted is to use the body line that runs the length of the car as my reference line for the graphic work (photo 8). That ensures that the graphic color lines stay straight along the sides of the car and enables me to continue this line forward once the hood is mounted.

Moving back to the graphic work on the sides of the car, the first color applied is HOK #KBC17 violette. This is a much

PHOTO 8: The body line visible just below the quarter glass runs the length of the body and will serve as the base line for laying out the graphics on the side of the car. That makes it very easy to continue this line forward once the hood has been installed.

PHOTO 9: The side of the car is masked in preparation for the first of the graphic colors, a light purple.

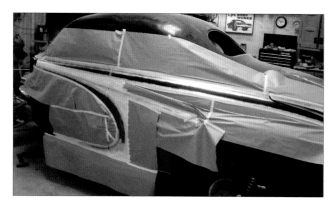

PHOTO 10: Most of the light purple is covered as the graphic layout work continues in anticipation of adding red stripes.

lighter purple than the deep purple used as a base color for the car. This purple is more akin to Chrysler's Plum Crazy purple. It goes on first because it is the more dominant of the two graphic colors. This color also mixes 2:1, two parts color to one part RU310 reducer, and I'll apply three medium-wet coats using the Binks M1-G with a 1.3 mm spray tip.

Notice in photo 9 that I have masked the side of the car, leaving exposed only those areas of the car that are to be sprayed KBC17 violette. Overspray will not be a factor, thus the reason for not masking the entire car.

The second color, KBC20, is the same color I used to paint the frame, and for the most part this color will be laid out in the form of stripes (photo 10). Notice that the edges around the tape lines appear to be blurry. I selected this shot to show you that sometimes what seems great on paper doesn't work out in real life. The blurred lines are caused from having air brushed a silver metallic paint around the edges of the light purple. The plan called for adding a 1/16-inch-wide silver accent line to the graphics. However, once the silver was on the car, I didn't like it. It detracted from the layout. Fortunately, removing the silver was a simple matter of spraying red base color over it.

How do I make my graphic lines sharp when adding colors to the car? I never use masking tape to lay out graphic work. I use 3M Scotch Fine Line Tape. This is a blue polypropylene film tape especially designed for multicolored separation. It leaves a nice, sharp line between the colors, with almost no chance of imprint damage when used over freshly painted surfaces. Fine Line is available in several widths, with the most popular widths being 1/16, 1/8, 1/4, and 1/2 inch.

So what does the car look like with the graphics on it? See for yourself (photo 11). I think the car is going to look great. All that is left for me to do now is add a single coat of clear over the graphic work to lock the colors down.

PHOTO 11: The completed graphic work. What's left to do now is add some clear over the graphic work.

NOTES

CHAPTER 16

THE FINAL
CLEAR COATS

When I left the shop last night, I had just completed the graphics work on the sides of the car and locked down those colors with a single coat of clear. To refresh your memory, I had only a twelve-hour window within which to apply the clear coat over my graphics colors, or I would have had to go back and sand those coats. Since the graphics colors are metallic, sanding would have cut into the metallic color and probably would have left a mottled and blotchy finish. That's not acceptable, so the only solution was to lock down the colors with a clear coat. I still have to lightly sand the clear coat applied over the graphics using 1000-grit sandpaper before I can apply the final clear coats, but that's better than sanding and reapplying the color coats.

BURYING PAINT LINES

Normally, I apply two additional coats of clear to the body, for a total of three coats, then bring out the 1000-grit sandpaper and start the sanding and polishing process. The cookie crumbs in this lemonade are those two additional graphics colors I applied to the car after applying the initial purple base coat. Those additional colors have created paint lines on the surface, and I don't want to be able to feel those lines once the car is finished.

In paint shop circles, we refer to the upcoming process to get rid of the paint lines as burying the colors. This is accomplished by literally piling on the clear coats to form a buildup of clear over the paint lines. Once the clear has cured, usually within forty-eight hours, it is aggressively sanded with 1000-grit sandpaper until the paint lines are no longer felt. That is how you "bury" paint lines.

PREPPING FOR THE FINAL CLEAR COATS

In photo 1, notice that I have once again removed the doors and the deck lid. This allows me to apply the clear coats evenly everywhere, including inside the door jambs and around the deck lid opening.

I haven't mentioned the need for masking the car because that part of the spraying process really hasn't been an issue. But now that the body is back on the frame, masking does become an issue. I can't take the chance of having the clear coats oversprayed onto the frame or the engine.

Clear coats are the worst when it comes to creating overspray. Spraying clear is like spraying enamel was in the old days. Anything that isn't masked off will receive overspray. To prevent overspray problems, I even go so far as to remove vehicles from the driveway in front of the shop for fear they will be coated.

As you can see in photo 1, I masked off the underside of the car, as well as the firewall and the engine, in order to prevent overspraying the frame. Recall that previously

PHOTO 1: The doors and deck lid are once again removed from the car. This allows better access to the door jambs and deck lid opening when spraying the clear coats.

I gave the firewall three coats of clear in anticipation of not having to deal with the task of spraying around the engine; thus the need for masking that part of the car now.

THE CLEAR COATING PROCESS

Clear coating the body starts with a thorough sanding. I very lightly wet sand every inch of the body using 1000-grit sandpaper on a soft foam block. Never, ever sand with your bare hands. Doing so can result in furrows on the surface that exactly match the size and shape of your fingers. Not a good thing to have on your ride.

What block am I using to sand the body? For this work, I prefer the 3M #5442, 5-inch-long foam block. I'm not looking to remove much of the clear that is already on the body; I just want to roughen up the surface enough to accept the additional coats. I do need to warn you that if the single coat of clear is sanded through and the color coat beneath is exposed, all bets are off and the exposed area must be correctly dealt with.

What does a sanded-through area look like? Unfortunately, I have a prime example (photo 2). Notice the change in color. It's that change in color that says the clear coat has been breached and the color coat beneath has been exposed.

How do you correctly deal with this type of problem? You can't simply add more clear to the spot. The color change will still be there. What must be done is to blend more color over the spot. But there's a catch. You cannot simply cover the sanded-through area with more color. The edges around the sand-through will wrinkle because the solvents in the fresh color coat will penetrate under the edges of the clear coat and lift it away from the surface. The exposed color coat must be sealed, in this case

by using HOK #KS10 sealer, then covered with additional color before adding the clear coat.

Getting back to the additional clear coats, the next step is a thorough cleaning. The painting area must be as clean as possible. That means sweeping and cleaning everywhere, then wetting everything down to help settle any dust that may still be lingering in the shop. After that, it is time for me to get clean. That means a new painting suit, latex gloves, and head sock (photo 3). What's not obvious in the photo is that I am wearing an Eastwood Pure Air 2000 breathing system #20397. This system uses a full face mask and provides fresh air for breathing when it's attached to the filtering unit.

I talked about the mixing ratios for the HOK products in chapter 15, so I won't cover that information again here. What I will talk about is the spray gun I'll be using. The gun of choice for spraying clear coats is the DeVilbiss GFG-670 Plus gravity feed gun. This is not an HVLP spray gun in that it requires higher air pressure than does a true HVLP, around 28 psi at the inlet. Even so, it produces great results. I'll be using a 1.3 mm spray tip.

CLEAR COAT APPLICATION

Back when I refinished Project Charger, each coat of clear was applied medium wet. The results were excellent, but the medium-wet coats left a surface that had a slight orange peel effect to it. To remove the orange

PHOTO 2: This light spot may look harmless. In reality, the clear coat has been removed in this area, and the color coat beneath has been exposed.

PHOTO 3: The well-dressed painter takes care of himself. I'm wearing a new painter's suit, latex gloves, head sock, and a full-face, fresh air intake respirator.

peel, I sanded every panel on that car until each one was as smooth as glass. Needless to say, I spent several days on the process.

Today, things are a little different. Since doing Project Charger, the paint manufacturers have made great strides toward improving their products. Colors are easier to spray, and clear coats no longer produce as much of the orange peel effect as they once did.

Spray gun manufacturers also stepped up to the plate and refined their products to the point that now a mere change in tip size can take a quality spray gun from laying down primer to laying down slick and smooth clear coats.

Of course, all of this improvement and refinement had to be dealt with in the paint shop. As products and tools change, so must the guy using these products and tools. So today, instead of applying three medium-wet coats, the way we did in the old days (last year), I start the clear coat application with a first coat that is best described as being somewhere between medium dry and medium wet.

There's no real trick to achieving this type of application. I just speed up the stroke of the gun during application. For example, in the old days, I would have taken about five seconds to move the length of this quarter panel when spraying a medium-wet coat. Today, I take about half that time to make this same spray pass. The result is an initial coat that at first glance appears far too thin and much too rough, as you can see in photo 4. Remember my warning about clear coat overspray being ubiquitous? That's it hanging in the air behind the car.

This coat of clear may look sparse, but take heart. As the coat begins to cure, it also begins to flow out, one of those improvements I talked about. It just needs a little drying time, about fifteen minutes at 70 degrees F, to flow out and lay flat. But then, fifteen minutes of drying time can seem like an eternity when you are staring at a clear coat you know is much too thin and far too rough. Getting antsy is a bad thing, though. The clock must tick down the fifteen minutes before the next coat can go on. If you don't wait, you risk getting runs and orange peel, and that's not good.

TICK TOCK, TICK TOCK

The second coat is applied slightly more slowly than the first. This is still not a medium-wet coat. I make this pass in three to four seconds. That's slower, but not much slower. Once this coat is on the panel, the difference in the surface is obvious. The clear has laid out smooth (photo 5), with no traces of orange peel anywhere.

Another fifteen minutes of cure time, and I'm ready for the third coat. But hold the phone. This next coat is not going over the entire body. This coat is for the graphics work on the sides of the car only. It is applied at the same speed the second coat was applied.

The idea here is to gain some depth to the clear coat in the areas that need depth, which is along the paint lines of the graphics work. This buildup of clear will help when it comes time to sand the paint lines smooth.

In the old days, I would have had concerns about leaving a dry edge along the length of the stripes when using this technique. Today, with the improved flow-out characteristics of the clear coats, leaving a dry edge is pretty much a thing of the past.

Thirty minutes later, I'm ready to apply a fourth coat. What happened to the fifteen minutes drying time between coats I used previously? At this point, I have a

PHOTO 4: The first coat of clear. From this angle, you can see how rough the coat appears. Within minutes this coat will begin to flow out and become smooth.

PHOTO 5: The second coat of clear goes on. Notice how the clear is beginning to lay flat and shine.

pretty good buildup of clear on the car. That buildup has trapped a lot of solvents within the layers of clear. Pausing to give the clear an extra fifteen minutes to cure helps dissipate those trapped solvents. What can happen if I don't give the clear coat that extra fifteen minutes of cure time? Solvent pops.

What's a solvent pop? Solvent pops look like tiny pinpricks all over the surface of the clear coat. Think about a sauce pan of pudding boiling on the stove. (Yep, my wife lets me lick the spoon. That's how I know about boiling pudding.) As the pudding boils, steam bubbles form on the bottom of the pan and move to the surface of the pudding, where they pop. Solvent pops happen the same way. They form at the bottom of the clear coat and move to the surface, where they dissipate.

The problem is that it can take some time for the solvents to work their way through multiple layers of clear and reach the surface. If the coats are applied too quickly, the solvents in the first coats may still be moving to the surface while the exposed surface of the fourth coat is drying and forming a skim. When those solvents from the first coats finally do move to the surface, they burst through the dried skim and leave behind holes in the clear coat. Normally, if you get one solvent pop, you get a few hundred. The only way to fix solvent pops is to allow the clear to cure, sand the surface smooth, and apply more clear. That's dollars spent and time wasted just because you were in a hurry to apply the next coat of clear.

Getting back to applying that fourth coat of clear, I spray the coat at the same speed I used to apply the second and third coats. I've still not slowed to the medium-wet application rate. But that's all right. The surface is looking nice.

How does the car look in photo 6? You can still see the haze of clear overspray hanging in the air, but the car looks great.

SANDING THE CLEAR COATS

A characteristic of clear coats is that the longer the finish cures, the harder it becomes. That's great when you think about the longevity this gives to the overall finish, but not so great when you think about the need to sand and compound a finish that is getting harder by the minute. I normally give a clear coat finish at least two days to cure before doing any sanding or compounding. That ensures

that the finish has had time to completely cure, yet still be soft enough to be easily sanded and compounded.

I'm using the deck lid for demonstration purposes as I go through the sanding and polishing procedures.

To start with, whatever you are sanding must be clean. This may seem like a no-brainer, but trust me, it is very important and quite often overlooked. Fresh clear coats are easily scratched, and the easiest way to scratch a fresh clear coat is to trap a piece of dirt or debris between the sandpaper and the clear coat. With that thought in mind, I always begin by washing the surface that is to be sanded.

Next, I need to think about sandpaper grits. Clear coats can tolerate sandpapers as coarse as 1000 grit, so that is where I begin. What if you use a coarser sandpaper? Don't. The next grade down is 800 grit, and using this sandpaper would result in a surface that is so rough, a heavy sanding with 1000 grit might not remove all of the scratch marks. The result might be the need to recoat the panel or the entire vehicle with more clear just to remove the sand scratches.

Once the panel has been thoroughly sanded using 1000 grit, I move up to 1500-grit and repeat the process. After that, it's on to 2000 grit for a final sanding in preparation for compounding.

Sounds easy, right? If only it was. Let's start by getting the terminology correct. In paint shop lingo, the sanding and polishing process is referred to as color sanding and buffing. So when I use that phrase, you will know what I'm talking about.

I always color sand by hand using a soft, round sanding pad, 3M #5291. This pad is specifically designed for use with 3M Hookit II sanding discs. The discs themselves are 3M #0869 1000 grit and 3M #0850 1500 grit. The 2000

PHOTO 6: The last coat of clear is on the car. The body really shines, and all that is left is a little compounding and polishing.

grit comes in 5½ x 9–inch sheets, 3M #02624, and is best used with the 3M #5442 Soft Hand Block.

The Hookit II disc can also be used on an orbital pneumatic palm sander, but unless you are proficient with one of these machines, I would not recommend its use, especially on a vehicle as rounded as the '46. What's rounded got to do with it? Pneumatic palm sanders have a flat sanding pad, and they work great on flat surfaces. It is much more difficult to get a flat pad to sand a curved surface without cutting deep into the clear coat. That deep cutting could actually go through the clear coat and expose the color coat beneath. That would call for more color and more clear; in other words, starting over.

Photo 7 is the deck lid after being sanded smooth using 1000-grit sandpaper. Notice that the shine is gone and the surface now has a very smooth, very dull sheen to it. That's the goal. Any imperfections left on the surface remain shiny; the dull sheen contrasts those imperfections.

Now look at the same surface after being sanded with 2000 grit (photo 8). I skipped the 1500-grit surface because it looks very much like the 1000-grit surface. The difference in the 2000-grit surface is obvious: it has taken the finish from very flat to almost shiny. Since bringing back the shine is the ultimate goal, completing the sanding process using 2000 grit is definitely worth the effort.

I could easily spend an hour compounding this panel to bring back the shine if I stopped sanding after using the 1000 grit. But by continuing the sanding process and finishing with 2000 grit, I can easily cut my buffing time in half. More time spent sanding, but less time spent buffing. It's a trade-off timewise, but less physical laborwise.

POLISHING THE CLEAR COAT

To bring back the shine, the machine of choice is a variable speed electrical buffer. Many professional shops prefer to use pneumatic buffers, and they work quite well. The difference is that professional shops have giant compressors that can handle the cfm requirements of a pneumatic buffer; most garage restorers do not.

Select a buffer with a top speed of around 3200 rpm. Anything faster is considered a grinder and should not be used as a buffer. High speed equals heat, and heat equals burned paint. Not a good combination.

> **TIP**
>
> *Always plug electric tools into GFI (ground fault interrupter) outlets. They will instantly stop the flow of electricity should the tool short out or should you venture into a puddle of water and act as a ground.*

Select a wool or wool blend buffing pad to start the polishing process. For this ride, I'm using the Liquid Ice Extra Cut Polishing System, Eastwood #25266. This package includes one quart of Liquid Ice Extra Cut Compound, a heavy-duty hook-and-loop backing pad that will attach to most buffers, a wool buffing pad to remove the sanding scratches left from the 2000 grit, a blue foam pad for removing swirl marks left from the wool buffing pad, and a white foam pad to produce a high-gloss finish (photo 9).

I begin the buffing process using the wool pad. I apply a small amount of Liquid Ice Compound to the surface and work in a roughly 2 x 2–foot area, never allowing the machine to sit in one spot for very long. Doing so

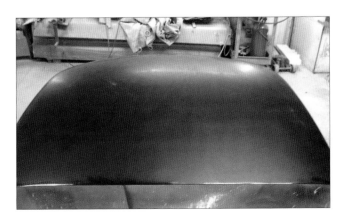

PHOTO 7: The deck lid has been sanded using 1000-grit sandpaper. The dull, flat surface is a good indicator that the panel has been thoroughly sanded.

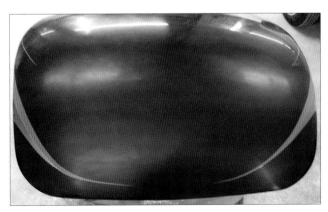

PHOTO 8: The same deck lid after being sanded using 2000 grit. Notice that the dull look is gone and the shine is beginning to return.

PHOTO 9: The Liquid Ice Polishing System is a great choice when it comes to bringing out the shine.

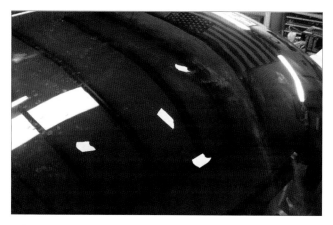

PHOTO 10: Imperfections found after the compounding process has been completed are marked using masking tape. Once marked, I can either sand them smooth or continue compounding the surface to remove them.

PHOTO 11: Now this is a shine. Anyone need a shave?

TIP

If the Liquid Ice Compound begins to dry, dampen the surface with a mist of clean water. Water reactivates the compound and extends the buffing time.

could create a buildup of heat that could burn the fresh clear coat.

I continue this process of working in small sections until the entire panel has been compounded and is free of all sanding scratches.

How do you know when the sanding scratches are gone? Sanding with the 2000 grit should have removed them, but if any are left, they will become visible as the shine begins to come out. Generally, a little extra compounding in the area of a found scratch will remove it. If not, it is back to the 2000-grit sandpaper.

Here's the trick. If I see a sand scratch or even a small imperfection in the surface after the area has been buffed, I first try applying more compound to the area and doing more buffing. If that doesn't remove the problem, I leave it and continue buffing the rest of the panel. Once the panel is completely buffed, I wash the panel with a solution of distilled water and 10 percent vinegar mixed in a spray bottle, and wipe the panel dry using a lint-free detail cloth. The water and vinegar solution act to remove any compound that might be trapped in a scratch and helps expose the problem. Once the scratches or imperfections are exposed, I mark each one using a small piece of masking tape (photo 10).

That saves me the trouble of having to search the panel a second time, looking for problem areas when I'm ready to remove them. Removal is accomplished via a spray bottle filled with water and a piece of 2000 grit on a block. I wet sand every imperfection and repeat the buffing and polishing process.

Next comes the blue foam pad. At this point, the panel should be looking nice. No more dull areas and no more sand scratches. This pad works best if dampened before use. Once damp, I apply several small drops of Liquid Ice directly to the pad, not to the surface being polished, then polish the surface until all traces of swirl marks have been removed.

Next comes the white foam pad. This pad also works best when damp. I apply several small drops of Liquid Ice to the pad and lightly polish the surface to bring out the shine. You should be able to shave from this shine (photo 11).

Can't get the buffer into the tight corners? Try the Eastwood #12815 Pneumatic 3" Sander & Polishing Kit. The 3-inch pads in this kit make reaching those hard-to-get-at areas much easier (photo 12).

PHOTO 12: These 3-inch wool pads can be used with a die grinder or drill to buff those areas the larger buffer can't reach.

PHOTO 13: Operating the buffer at a slight tilt offers greater control over the machine.

PHOTO 14: Protecting the edges of the panel being buffed prevents the buffer from cutting through the paint on these delicate areas.

Here are some buffing tips:

- Never operate the buffer with the pad lying flat on the panel. Always slightly tip up the machine (photo 13). This method gives you better control over the machine and concentrates the polishing into a smaller, easy-to-monitor area.
- Use masking tape to protect all edges of the panel being polished (photo 14).
- Always drape the electrical cord over your shoulder when operating a buffer. This ensures that the cord will never become tangled in the machine.
- Wear eye protection and a NIOSH-approved dust mask, Eastwood #13000, when operating any type of buffer.
- Wash the car again before leaving for the day. Compound tends to sling everywhere when you're buffing. Compound left on a fresh clear coat can etch the surface, creating more work to remove the etching marks.
- Ask your paint supplier for a painter's smock. He should stock them, and they work great for keeping compound off of your clothing.

NOTES

NOTES

CHAPTER 17

THE
BUILDUP BEGINS

Although I still have paint work to do to this ride, such as refinishing the hood and front fenders, I'm going to stop the painting process for a little while and take care of some other aspects of this build. Once that is done, I'll paint the front-end parts and install them.

INSTALLING THE PAINLESS PERFORMANCE WIRING KIT

I don't like the idea of having to lean over freshly painted fenders to complete the necessary wiring, engine, and steering work that needs to be done to this car before I can turn the key and take the '46 for a spin. Taking care of these issues now, before the fenders are installed, will ensure that I don't end up leaning on my fresh paint. I'll start with the wiring and bring out the Painless Performance Products wiring kit ordered earlier.

The heart of the electrical system is an 18-circuit harness designed to accommodate all of the power accessories planned for this car, and then some. This harness is also available in a 12-circuit version for cars with fewer accessories, but as you may already know, project cars are always in flux. Extra circuits can often be a real gift when adding goodies to the ride.

If you read the fine print on the harnesses available from Painless, you will find two types of universal harnesses. One is configured for a column-mounted ignition switch, and the other is configured for a dash-mounted ignition switch. The harness I ordered is configured for a dash-mounted ignition switch. I'm not too keen on a column-mounted ignition switch in a street rod; it looks too modern for my taste.

WIRING TIPS

I can't take you through the entire installation procedure wire by wire, so what I'm going to do is offer a number of tips, suggestions, and methods I used to wire this car.

To start, Painless Performance has been at this for a number of years, so you can trust that when you purchase one of its products, it is going to work. If you do have a problem with one of the kits, more than likely the guys at

Painless have already found a cure for it. Go to the Web site or call the tech line. I promise you won't be stuck on hold for hours on end, and the tech guys can help you fix just about anything that can go wrong with the installation of one of their electrical systems.

When you open the 18-circuit harness box, the first thing to look for is the wire harness installation instructions. On page 1, you will find the wiring group headings Engine/Headlight Group, Dash Group, and Rear Light Group. Read each group's section thoroughly to familiarize yourself with the product before you do anything else.

After reading all three sections, lay out the new harness and separate it into the three sections (photo 1). You'll notice in the photo that all three sections key off of the fuse block. That means that every circuit in this harness is fused to protect the system should a short occur.

The next step is to determine where best in the car to route each group of wires and to establish a plan for wiring each individual electrical component in the car. This is basically roughing out the wiring, and if there is one thing you should know, it's that each group of wires

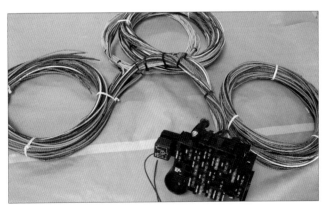

PHOTO 1: Wiring begins by familiarizing yourself with the different aspects of the main harness. Here I have separated the harness into the three main sections: the headlights, dash, and rear body.

must be routed in an area where possible damage to the wires can be eliminated. That means if the wires must be routed under the carpet, you should place them next to the console or out near the scuff plates, not in the open, where foot traffic or seat tracks might eventually degrade the wires and create a short circuit.

REAR LIGHT AND DASH GROUP

I elected to route the rear light group through the center console, then divide the group so that the wires operating the electrical components on the right side of the car are routed over to the right quarter panel, and the wires operating the electrical components on the left side of the car are routed over to the left quarter panel. From the quarter panels, I can route wires into each door (suicide opening), up to the roof panel for a dome light, and toward the rear of the car for taillights.

The dash group is self-explanatory as to where these wires belong. Incorporated in the dash group are the fuse panel, gauge wiring, wiper circuit, headlight switch circuit, and steering column circuit. The steering column circuit includes components such as the turn signals, emergency flashers, headlight dimmer switch (on some columns), and horn button.

Breaking down the components of the dash group further, I mount the fuse panel on the firewall just to the left of the steering column. For the time being, I leave the gauge wiring circuit stuffed into the area above the steering column so that the wiring will be there, ready for mounting once I'm ready to install the dash gauges.

The remaining dash group circuits, such as the headlight switch, wiper switch, and steering column wiring, will be routed to their proposed locations and left there until later.

THE ENGINE/HEADLIGHT GROUP

This is the meat of the wiring harness, as it controls the headlights, park lamps, front turn signal lamps, electric cooling fan, electric fuel pump, and everything else engine related. This part of the harness also contains the firewall pass-through bulkhead plug that allows the harness to transition from the dash area to the engine compartment. Painless provides a template, found at the back of the instruction manual, to use for cutting this opening.

Breaking down an 18-circuit harness into individual circuits and then wiring each one can be a daunting task, especially if this is your first time wiring a car. To help with that, Painless provides detailed instructions throughout the manual and a variety of basic schematics to help lead you through the process. The schematics are found near the back of the manual and will provide you with specific information on each circuit, including the number and color for each wire required for that circuit.

If, after reading the manual and checking out the schematics, you still aren't sure where a particular wire goes, refer to the chart at the very back of the manual. An example is wire #901. This is an 18-gauge, gray wire with a white tracer stripe that starts at the engine cooling fan switch and goes to the fan relay. If you have your glasses on, you can even read the words Fan Relay printed on the wire.

Every wire in the harness is color coded, numbered, and named in the same manner. That makes finding a specific wire a simple matter of checking the color, reading the number, then identifying the wire by name. It beats the heck out of crawling through the car trying to follow a wire back to its source.

If you like to test your work as you go along, I suggest starting with the charging circuit so you can begin to power up the car using a battery charger as the voltage source. This is part of the engine/headlight group and includes wiring for parts such as the battery, starter, and alternator. Forget about using the battery as the voltage source; it cranks out too many amps and could easily fry a few wires should you hook something up wrong. Once the charging circuit is up and running, it is a simple matter of moving through each remaining circuit until the car is completely wired.

Here are the tools you'll need:

- **Crimping tool:** Use a good-quality crimping tool to avoid overcrimping the terminals.

- **Wire stripper:** This is often a two-in-one tool provided with the crimping tool.

- **Test light:** I use both a test light and a voltmeter. The test light tells you if the circuit has power. The voltmeter will tell you if the circuit is receiving the correct voltage should the circuit require less than the normal 12 volts.

- **Hole saw:** I use a hole saw kit purchased from the local home improvement center. The kit contains various hole saw sizes and is capable of cutting thin metal.

- **Battery charger:** This is a very important tool, as it is used to provide voltage for testing various circuits. A 10-amp, or less, charger is recommended.
- **Heat-shrink tubing:** Purchase this product at the local home improvement center, and use it to cover and protect every terminal in all circuits. This not only decreases the chances of grounding problems later on but also gives your work a more professional appearance.

TIP

Neatness counts when wiring a car. Use wire ties, electrical tape, or harness wrap to bundle and contain loose wires.

AFFORDABLE FUEL INJECTION

Early into this project, I made the decision to toss the carburetor and go with a more up-to-date fuel management system. With gasoline prices always on the rise, the decision just made good sense.

I opted for an Affordable Fuel Injection system (photo 2). This is a multi-port fuel injection (MPFI) unit, which I selected because I wanted a great-looking unit that could be installed without a hitch and could pass for a carburetor sitting atop the engine at quick glance. Once I install a chrome air breather on top of this unit, it will be hard to tell that this is not a carburetor.

The best thing about selecting a unit from Affordable is that the unit is set up specifically for the engine being used. What does that mean? I gave the engine specifications, camshaft specifications, and desired performance specifications to the guys at Affordable, and they built and calibrated the unit to fit my car. I don't need a laptop with graphs I can't decipher or a travel agent to entice someone into coming to the shop just to make my car run. All I need to do is follow the easy-to-read instructions, and all will be well.

Of course, there are other considerations to work out when installing a fuel injection unit. Take a look at photo 3. These are some of the other components that come with the kit, and they include an ECM (electronic control module), distributor, wiring harness, fuel pump, fuel pressure regulator, and various sensors.

Some of these remaining components, such as the distributor, wiring harness, and sensors, can be installed on the engine now. The ECM box will need to be mounted somewhere under the dash, and a hole will need to be drilled through the firewall to route the wiring harness from the engine to the ECM. These are considerations that I will have to delay until I have more of the dash assembled. I can't afford to drill any holes in the firewall that might interfere with the mounting of something else, nor can I mount the ECM until I know where it will fit best. I'm thinking that the ideal location will be behind the old glove box location and just above the heater box.

Installation always starts with reading the instruction manual. Once you've read it, you'll wonder why you ever tolerated a carburetor. The manual is thorough, and every component is connector coded so you can't mess things up. It took me only a couple of hours to make the installation, and all I'll have to do later is provide a 12-volt source to the ECM and the fuel pump.

PHOTO 2: This is the heart of the Affordable Fuel Injection setup. I selected this unit because of its great looks.

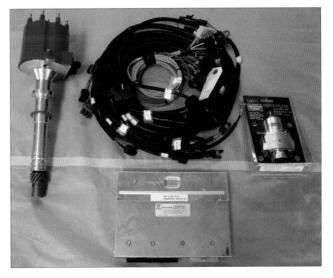

PHOTO 3: The heart of my Affordable Fuel Injection setup can't beat without these additional components. They include an ECM, distributor, wiring harness, fuel pump, fuel pressure regulator, and various sensors.

STEERING THE CAR

Routed between the steering wheel and the rack and pinion unit is a steel shaft that snakes its way through the firewall, down past the left-hand exhaust pipe, and alongside the frame rail. This is by no means a straight line, so I'll need to add at least two universal joint–type couplers to get the shaft to bend where necessary.

PHOTO 4: This universal joint is used to make bends in the steering column shaft to help snake the shaft through the various obstacles in the engine compartment.

PHOTO 5: This bearing block helps stabilize the steering shaft as it exits the firewall.

PHOTO 6: This vibration-dampening coupling separates the rack and pinion from the steering shaft. This prevents road vibration from telegraphing through the rack and pinion and traveling up the steering shaft to the steering wheel.

I don't want either of the bends to be sharp bends. Sharp bends can affect the way the car steers by creating stress points at the universal joint couplers. These stress points are hard spots in an otherwise free-turning steering wheel. To prevent this kind of problem, I want to make certain my bends are at 30 degrees or less.

It won't present a problem with this unit, but occasionally it is necessary to add more than two universal joint couplers to join the steering column to the rack and pinion unit. When that becomes necessary, a pillow block, or bearing-mounted support bracket, must be added to the shaft assembly to ensure that the assembly is completely stable. Three universal joint couplers can cause the steering shaft to wobble when turned. That's not acceptable.

To make up the shaft extending from the steering column down to the rack and pinion unit, I start with a 24-inch-long, ¾-inch-diameter DD shaft and cut it into one stick measuring 12 inches long and another stick measuring 14 inches long. What is a DD shaft, and where do you purchase this product? The DD stands for "double D," and that describes the cross sectional shape of the shaft. This is a very common steel steering shaft used to make up steering links between the steering wheel and the steering gear box or rack and pinion unit. I found several sources for both the shaft and the universal joints on eBay.

To make the bends in the shaft, I use universal joints designed specifically for this purpose (photo 4). One other piece I need to add to ensure that the shaft remains stable is a bearing block bolted to the firewall where the shaft exits (photo 5).

Finally, I add a vibration-dampening coupling at the rack and pinion (photo 6). This coupling separates the shaft from the rack and pinion to prevent road vibration from telegraphing up through the shaft to the steering wheel.

The last thing I can do with the steering is center the steering wheel. This is by no means a way to align the front suspension; rather, what I am doing is verifying that the suspension work already performed has been done correctly and that all will go well when I deliver the '46 to the front-end alignment shop for an alignment. This requires raising the front of the car with a floor jack and moving the jack stands to a point under the frame just behind the front wheels so the spindles move freely.

I start by turning the steering wheel full right, and then I turn the wheel left, counting the revolutions until the steering wheel stops. That's two-and-a-half turns. Now I divide that in half, which equals one-and-three-quarters turns. Then, I turn the steering wheel back one-and-three-quarters turns to center it.

The front brake rotor discs should be pointed straight ahead. If they're not, I use the tie-rod end adjustments at the rack and pinion to adjust each spindle one at a time until the rotors are pointed straight ahead. I tighten the adjustment nuts to secure the tie-rods. The steering wheel is centered as best can be without the aide of a pro.

The last concern here is to be sure the turn signal switch in the steering column operates correctly. To do that, I flip the switch lever down, turn the steering wheel to the right a half turn, then return the wheel to center. The switch lever should click and return to the off position. I repeat this procedure to the left. The switch lever should click and return to the off position.

Next on the list is the power steering pump. I elected to use a Saginaw brand pump. This pump was standard equipment on GM products for many years and will work quite well with my rack and pinion unit. The only catch here is coupling the Ford rack and pinion unit to the GM steering pump.

To accomplish this marriage, I began with a visit to my favorite automotive reclamation center in search of mounting brackets for the pump. While there, I scavenged the high-pressure line from a salvage Saginaw pump. I also visited the Ford section of the reclamation center and scavenged both the high- and low-pressure lines from the rack and pinion unit on an '82 Thunderbird. Am I about to install worn-out power steering fluid lines on the '46? No, I'm not. I just want to be sure these are the correct size lines and that they will screw into my rack and pinion unit and my power steering unit. When I know the lines fit, by screwing the lines into my rack and pinion, I'll take them to my local hydraulic line manufacturer and have them construct new lines to fit my married components. Used power steering pump? No. Remanufactured units are available at most automotive parts stores, and, if desired, chrome-plated pumps are available from several hot rod parts providers.

NOTES

_____

_____

_____

_____

_____

_____

_____

_____

CHAPTER 18

THE
BUILDUP CONTINUES

I n the previous chapter, I took care of a number of basic car-building issues that had to be accomplished before I could get serious about assembling this ride. With those issues out of the way, it is time to complete the painting process and begin the final buildup. I'll start by getting some color on the front sheet metal pieces.

PAINTING THE FRONT END

The front end appears to consist of two fenders, a hood, and a grille. But when you break down the front end sheet metal section of this car into individual pieces, it actually consists of ten parts: the hood, both fenders, two fender skirts, an upper radiator shield, a lower radiator shield, two side shields for the radiator, and a grille assembly. Luckily, the hood is the only part of this section that requires more than a single color. That means I can give the remaining nine parts a coat of sealer, three coats of under base black, three coats of purple, and three coats of clear, then install them on the car. The hood will get a single coat of clear, after which I'll install it and complete the graphics work begun earlier.

In photo 1, you can see I've already painted the fenders and hood and have mounted them on the car. That allows me to complete the graphics work by laying out the tape lines for the red and light purple accent colors (photo 2). The tape lines extend from the cowl, down the length of the hood where they will turn down and taper to a point near the front (photo 3).

Next, I mask off the hood and spray on the two colors (photo 4). Notice that I don't bother to remove the hood before applying these colors. Base colors don't tend to overspray the way clear coats do, so I don't have to worry about getting the red or light purple on my dark purple.

When the accent colors are dry enough for the hood to be safely handled, in about two hours, I remove the hood, return it to the spray booth, and give it three more coats of clear. Once that is done, I call the painting portion of this project done.

THE ASSEMBLY BEGINS

Assembly begins by adding more insulation. I know I've already given this ride some serious insulation using the

PHOTO 1: The front fenders are mounted back on the car.

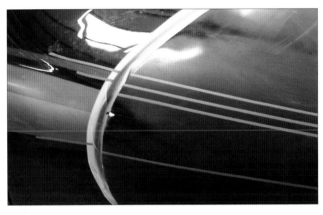
PHOTO 2: With the fenders and hood mounted on the car, I can lay out the tape lines to complete the graphics work.

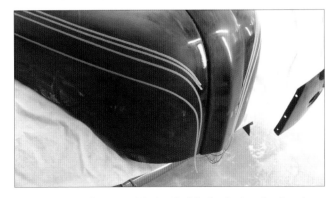
PHOTO 3: The tape lines extend the length of the hood, where they turn downward and taper to a point.

PHOTO 4: The graphics colors are added to complete the look.

PHOTO 5: Now is the time for adding additional insulation padding to the firewall, before the Hot Rod Air unit is hung in place.

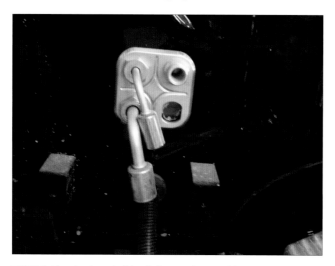

PHOTO 6: The aluminum bulkhead plate used to transition the heater and air conditioner lines from the engine compartment to the interior is mounted to the firewall.

LizardSkin products, but this is a completely different type of insulation. This insulating material is referred to in the upholstery business as rebond. It can consist of scraps of cotton cloth bonded together into a thick padding or be made of scrap foam bonded into sheets. The cotton cloth version can be found under the carpet of just about any factory vehicle on the road. The foam version is most often found in hot rods or under carpeting in the home. Either of these products works great in cars. I elected to go with the foam version because this is what my local upholstery trim shop sells, and it is very easy to cut and install.

Why add more insulation? Actually, I'll be blanketing the entire cab of this ride with rebond in anticipation of finishing things off with a little trim. It will add to the quiet inside of the car.

I had to think about the additional insulation now because I'm ready to install both the wiper motor and the heater unit under the dash. Once these parts have been mounted, there is no way I'd be able to access the firewall area behind them in order to cover it with rebond. Adding the extra insulation behind these components will have a muting effect on the noise from the wiper mechanisms and the blower motor.

To install the foam insulation, I use 3M Super Trim Adhesive Yellow #8090 and coat both the insulation and the firewall, including the underside of the cowl panel. The Super Trim Adhesive is basically a contact adhesive, so I allow it to dry to the touch before pressing the insulation into place.

With the insulation in place, I mount the windshield wiper motor and the Hot Rod Air heating and air conditioning unit to the cowl behind the dash (photo 5). I also take the time to route the defroster duct work, the condensation drain hose for the Hot Rod Air unit, and the bulkhead plate that transitions the air conditioning hoses from the engine compartment to the interior compartment (photo 6).

The refrigerant hoses that come with the Hot Rod Air kit are in bulk length and therefore must be cut to fit. The connector ends must be crimped on (photo 7), which is not a do-it-yourself project.

Mark the position of the connector ends on each hose before sending them out for crimping. I use a length of masking tape to mark each hose (photo 8). This ensures that each connector is facing the right direction and that the hoses do not have to be twisted to make the connections. Twisting can reduce the life of a hose.

The first thing I do is install the connector ends to the unit mounted under the dash, the bulkhead plate, the dryer, the compressor, and the condenser. Next, I measure for the hose lengths needed to join all of the components and cut the hoses to length. Once that is done, I deliver the hoses—there are six of them—to my local automotive air conditioner specialist and have the connectors crimped to the hoses.

Hose installation is a matter of installing the O-rings provided in the kit onto each of the connectors and assembling the pieces. What I won't do at this time is evacuate the system and add a charge of R134a refrigerant. I'll save that until I have the car running.

CONTROLS AND OUTLETS

Inside the car, I have a couple of cosmetic considerations to think about when it comes to delivering that crisp, cold air to the occupants. First is where to locate the controls. The control panel that comes with the kit is pretty basic and is designed for mounting underneath the dash. I elect to modify the control panel and incorporate it into the dash (photo 9). That will make the controls easy to reach and extremely functional.

Next, I have to think about where to position the duct outlets. The outlets are nice-looking pieces and will look good no matter where I place them. The only condition for placement is that the outlets be mounted so that each one—and there are four of them—can be easily directed toward the occupants. Recall that in my chat with the guys at Hot Rod Air, I learned that air conditioning works best when the outlets are directed at the car's occupants.

This is something that I gave some serious thought to earlier in the project. I knew I wanted the face of the dash to be uncluttered, so I didn't want to try to mount all four outlets to that panel. Instead, I elected to place two of the outlets near the center of the dash, as seen in photo 9, and the other two below the dash on each cowl post (photo 10).

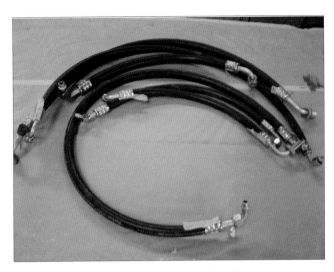

PHOTO 7: The air conditioner hoses are cut to length and the end connectors are crimped on.

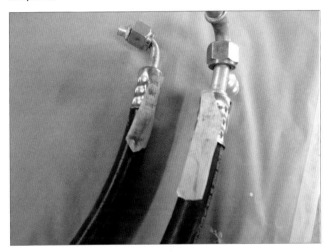

PHOTO 8: The fittings are marked with masking tape to ensure that each one is in the correct position when the hoses are crimped. Notice that the professionals doing the crimping left the masking tape in place as they crimped the hoses. That ensures that the fitting is pointing in the right direction.

PHOTO 9: I elect to modify the control unit for the Hot Rod Air unit and mount it in the dash. Also notice the two center-mounted duct outlets. These are part of the kit and add a nice touch to the finished dash.

PHOTO 10: I decided to mount the other two ducts just below the dash on the cowl posts. It helps maintain that uncluttered look of the dash.

PHOTO 11: In keeping with the overall theme of the rest of the car, the dash is left clean and uncluttered.

PHOTO 12: The gauges are Auto Meter. The nostalgic look is in keeping with the old-school theme of the car and really does the dash justice.

Where did I get the dash? This is a shop-made unit. I used the original dash as a template and constructed this dash out of fiberglass. I gave the new dash a sloping top, in keeping with the shape of the original dash, and a flat front (photo 11). The flat front gives the dash that clean and uncluttered look I'm looking for and provides an excellent platform upon which I can mount the gauges and switches.

The gauges are from the Auto Meter Street Rod Arctic White series (photo 12) and consist of a tachometer, speedometer, fuel gauge, oil pressure gauge, temperature gauge, volt gauge, and a clock. A clock? You bet. The clock helps balance the gauges across the dash, and since it is made by Auto Meter, it matches the other gauges.

The dash is refinished in a metallic gray to coordinate with the gray interior colors and is accented by the red band seen across the bottom. The red band is there to bring the outside graphics work into the car and will be continued onto the doors in the form of red vinyl trim once I reach that point in the build.

BLEEDING THE BRAKES

One last detail I attend to before mounting the dash panel in the car is to bleed the brakes. The master cylinder is located behind the dash, and once the dash panel is installed, bleeding the brakes and adding more brake fluid will be difficult.

To bleed the brakes, I start by filling the reservoir with new fluid. Next, I attach a handheld pump–style bleeding device to the right rear brake caliper, and pump until the fluid flows without any air bubbles. Then, I move to the left rear caliper and repeat the process.

After that, I move to the right front, repeat, then finish with the left front. This sounds easy, and it is. The only thing to remember is to check the fluid level in the reservoir periodically, as it holds only so much fluid and must be refilled as necessary. I know the brakes are bled when I have a full brake pedal that holds solid when I put some weight on it.

The brake pedal feels spongy? There is a leak in the system somewhere. The easiest way to find a leak is to clean the floor, press the brake pedal for a minute or so, then exit the car and look for the puddle of brake fluid. More than likely you will find the puddle at one of the brake calipers, and more than likely the leak is a result of a loose connection.

MOUNTING THE DASH

With the brake work completed, the dash can then be mounted in the car. Since I used the old dash as a template, the new dash uses the same attachment points as the old dash and is easily bolted into place. Here's a good tip if you have ever tried to wire gauges while lying flat on your back reaching up into the dark recesses of a dash panel: try prewiring the gauges and incorporating a plug-in connector to connect the gauges to the wiring harness. Where do you find a ten- to twelve-wire connector? Try a GM steering column wiring connector; it has provisions for connecting up to fifteen wires.

GLASS INSTALLATION

With the top on the '46 being chopped a full 3 inches, picking up the phone or dialing up the Internet in search of glass is basically a waste of time. Without a doubt, I can find and purchase new glass to fit a stock 1946 Ford Business Coupe, but ordering glass to fit my 3-inch chop would be like ordering steak at the local snack-in-a-sack eatery. You're just not going to like what you get. I have to find someone who can custom cut new glass to fit this ride.

I browsed the Internet and found several sources that can cut laminated glass to fit just about anything. The problem is that they are relying on my ability to measure and correctly template the glass openings so that the glasses can be cut to the correct sizes. In some worlds, that may be great; in my world, things often go wrong, and when they do I usually find myself back at square one wondering where they went wrong.

It's the wondering where things went wrong part of that scenario that prompts me to call my local glass guy and have him come by the shop. Recall that earlier I talked to my glass guy and placed my name on his job list. He's been waiting for my call and is ready to help me out.

Remember the saying about good cooks: When the chef turns on the stove, your job is to sit in the corner and peel the potatoes. Good glass guys are the same way. They'd rather you go somewhere else and peel potatoes while they work. It results in far less glass breakage.

Starting at the rear of the car, the back glass is completely stock and needs only a new rubber gasket to hold it in place. Steele Rubber provided me with an exact factory duplicate gasket. Since this is a stock-size replacement glass, it came as a clear glass. To get it to match the side windows, which will be cut from dark tinted glass, my glass guy took the time to apply a tinting film to the glass before installing it (photo 13).

As mentioned above, the side glasses for the '46 are dark tinted (photo 14), and were cut from laminated sheet glass. The actual method used to cut the glass is somewhat of a secret, but as I understand it the process is similar to the sandblasting method used to engrave stone. But what do I know? Since the quarter glass is stationary, the installers set this glass in urethane. It isn't coming out, ever.

The door glasses need to move up and down and so are urethane set in the power window run channel.

The windshield consists of two pieces of flat, laminated glass cut and beveled so that the pieces can be butt-joined in the middle. I've seen a number of hot rods with no center-mounted vertical bar between the two pieces of glass. It's a good look, but I believe the seal between the two glasses is made using clear silicone.

PHOTO 13: The back glass is completely stock and is installed using a new rubber gasket from Steele Rubber. The only change was to have the glass tinted before installation.

PHOTO 14: All of the side glass is dark tinted. This is basically the same tint shade you'll find in the Chevrolet Suburban side windows.

That works great for a while, but sooner or later the silicone will break down from exposure to UV radiation, turn yellow, and have to be replaced. To avoid this problem, I elect to use a narrow black plastic strip as a vertical bar. It has a very clean look to it, and, since it is urethane set into place, it will be there forever, no digging it out to replace it when it degrades.

As for installation, the installers wrap a black plastic beading that measures ½ inch wide around each windshield glass, then urethane set the glasses into place one at a time (photo 15).

The center bar, which is a ⅜-inch-wide strip of black plastic, is urethane glued between the two glasses only after the two windshield halves are in place. How does the new windshield look? Not bad. The plastic beading may be there to help hold the windshield halves in place, but it really gives the installation a very professional look (photo 16).

PHOTO 15: The windshield halves are set in place one at a time. Notice the black beading surrounding the glass and the masking tape to help hold the glass in place until the urethane sets.

PHOTO 16: The center bar is almost invisible, and the final product looks great.

NOTES

_____

_____

_____

_____

_____

_____

_____

_____

NOTES

CHAPTER 19

INTERIOR TRIM

When it comes to installing interior trim, you really have only two options: do the work yourself, or have someone else do the work.

In the restoration world, doing the work yourself usually means browsing a few catalogs for replacement door panels, headliners, seat covers, and carpeting, then doing the install yourself. However, in the "it ain't strictly stock" world of automotive construction, it isn't likely you will be able to earmark items on catalog pages, where all you need to decide upon is the color of the trim. I'm not aware of any company making headliners tailored to fit chopped tops or carpet kits designed to work with shop-engineered driveshaft tunnels. That's when do-it-yourself takes on a whole new meaning, and having someone else do it can suddenly seem like the best idea.

TURNING TO THE PROS

OK, let's consider turning this project over to a professional and having him do the interior. The first step is to find a qualified trim shop. That starts with a visit to the shop of choice and having a short chat with the owner. Remember, his time costs money; ask your questions, then be quiet and listen to what he has to say.

What questions are you going to ask? Ask for references you can go look at, then get in the car and go look. If the price of gasoline prohibits a trip down the road, ask to tour the shop to see what is being worked on at that moment. Most shops are happy to show off their work. Just don't be surprised if they are reluctant to have you walking around the shop alone: insurance is very costly, and safety is paramount. When you do get to see their work, look for details such as straight seam lines and trim panels that fit. Like everything else, quality shows through, and you'll know almost immediately if the shop is worth consideration. While you are looking at their work, take a moment to look over the shop. Is it clean? Do the project cars appear to be well cared for? That's two more telltale signs that the shop cares about its customers.

Then ask about scheduling. Most good trim shops are busy, very busy. They may install only one or two full interiors at a time, and each one may take months to complete. Be ready to get in line. For example, I signed up for a convertible top replacement in June, delivered the car to the trim shop in August, and picked up the car in November. That's five months to do what I thought would be a simple job. How was I to know?

Then there is the big question: how much? OK, it varies. If you want leather, expect to pay more, much more. If you want vinyl that looks like leather, you'll pay a little less. Is leather better? Yes and no. Leather is considered to be the top of the heap in custom interiors. You just can't beat the look and feel of genuine leather. On the flip side, leather seats look great for a while, then they begin to show wear in the form of wrinkles and shiny spots. Leather also stains; vinyl doesn't. Consider that if you have grandkids just waiting to take a spin in the new ride.

CUSTOMIZING THE INTERIOR YOURSELF

Didn't know the trim guys charged that much? Now you do. So what's left? What if I told you there is a way for you to install the interior in your ride without spending a fortune on sewing equipment? I thought you might be interested. Let's give it a try.

The first thing you need is a plan. Custom interiors don't just happen; they are planned down to the last detail, then constructed according to that plan. The second thing you need is something with which to construct the interior.

What's the plan for this car, and how did I arrive at such a layout? The plan calls for a vinyl interior using three different colors of material. The two base colors, a light gray and a darker gray, were derived from the colors in the seats. Recall that I lucked into finding seats for the '46 on one of my excursions to the automotive reclamation center. Those seats are two-tone gray.

The third color is red. This will be used as an accent color and will coordinate with the red band on the dash to bring the red exterior graphics color into the car. This keeps the flow of the car in tune and, as my artistic mother would have put it, "completes the touch."

The material list consists of vinyl trim, foam padding, a suitable backing material, and something from which to make templates. I'll go into more detail about these materials as I move deeper into the process. Right now, I need to complete my plan. It is hard to order materials if you don't know how much you need.

DOOR TRIM PANELS

Look through the window of any street rod, and the first pieces of interior trim you will see is the opposite door trim panel. Since this is the first part of the interior seen, this is also the best place to begin the interior trim scheme layout (photo 1). I use heavy cardboard to make my templates, which will serve as the drawing boards for laying out the interior design. How heavy is the cardboard? In print shop terms, it is 25 point. In body shop terms, it is .025 inch thick.

I've taken the time to carefully trim and fit the pieces to the door and quarter panel. Each piece will be used as the pattern for the real trim panels once I've

finished laying out the scheme. You'll notice from all of the drawing in photo 1 that I had several fits and starts before I arrived at a final layout.

To explain what I've come up with here, the area of the templates covered with masking tape denotes the placement of the red stripe. This stripe actually begins on the dash panel and will flow across the door and end on the quarter panel trim piece. Notice that the stripe gets progressively wider as it moves toward the rear of the passenger compartment. Parallel lines are very difficult to construct and can detract from the looks of the car if not done right. Allowing the red band to widen as it moves rearward eliminates that problem.

ARMRESTS

Just below the red stripe on the door panel, I penciled in the position of the armrest. Since the bulk of this trim panel will be covered with the light gray material, I'll cover the armrest with the darker gray. As I did with the red stripe, I'll let the darker gray material continue on and move across the quarter panel trim piece.

Referring back to the armrest, the location of this piece on the door isn't random. Measure any vehicle door out there, and you will find the armrest is normally located 8 to 9 inches below the door glass belt line and starts roughly at the halfway point across the door, where it extends back toward the rear edge of the door. This armrest will be placed about 8 inches below the belt molding, but I'm going to move it closer to the front of the door so I can add a handhold. This forward positioning of the armrest plus the addition of the handhold will provide a good place to grab the door and pull it shut.

PHOTO 1: Every interior panel starts with a template. Here I've constructed cardboard templates for the right door and quarter panel.

PUTTING IT ALL TOGETHER

All of the panels made for this car will be constructed using the techniques described below. The only changes will be the size and mounting locations of each of the panels.

Working first with the door trim panel, I start by cutting the base panel from a sheet of lauan. This is a type of thin plywood, about 3/16 inch thick, which is available at most home improvement centers. The base panel is cut according to my template using a jigsaw and then attached to the door with a couple of sheet metal screws (photo 2). The screws allow me to correctly position the base panel on the door no matter how many times I remove it to refine the fit.

How do I refine the fit? I use a belt sander or hand sanding blocks to remove any part of the trim panel that doesn't fit right. What's a good fit? In this case, a good fit means locating the trim panel 1/4 inch inboard of the door frame all around the door.

Once the fit is correct, I add plastic push-in retainers around the perimeter of the trim panel as a means of final attachment (photo 3). These are Crest Industries #15866 retainers and measure 5/16 inch in diameter by 1 1/16 inch in length (photo 4). They are the same style GM has used to attach door trim panels for more than twenty years.

To install the retainers, I drill 1/4-inch-diameter holes through both the base panel and the door frame, then push the retainers through the holes. The holes are spaced about 6 inches apart around the perimeter of the door.

The next step is to construct the armrest (photo 5). The base is cut from the sheet of lauan, and the top is cut from 1/2-inch-thick plywood. The top is glued and screwed to the baseplate using carpenter's glue and #8 x 1-inch wood screws. How did I determine the size and shape of the baseplate? Go back and look at the template on the door in photo 1. The base of the armrest is drawn out and marked Arm Rest. The size and shape are a result of my trial and error designing.

The handhold in the armrest is an oval slot cut into both the baseplate and the top. The edges of the slot are rounded off to improve comfort when gripping the armrest. What's a good length for a handhold? It just needs to be large enough to accommodate all four fingers comfortably. In my case, that's about 4 inches.

After the glue dries overnight, I finish the armrest by covering it with cardboard. This is the same material I

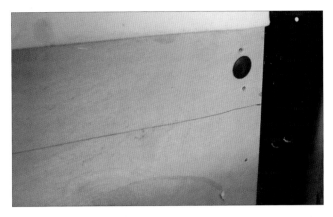

PHOTO 2: The base of the new trim panel is attached to the door, then carefully trimmed until the fit is just right.

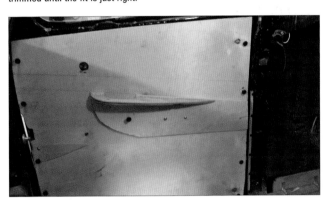

PHOTO 3: The trim panel is held in place using these plastic push-in retainers spaced about 6 inches apart around the perimeter of the door.

PHOTO 4: Door trim panels must be removable. These GM-style plastic push-in clips from Crest Industries are used to secure the panel to the door.

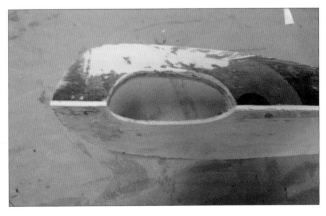

PHOTO 5: The base for my armrest is cut from a sheet of lauan, and the top plate is cut from 1/2-inch plywood. Notice the oval slot. This will become a handhold.

used to make the templates, and it will span the gap between the outer edge of the top piece and the bottom of the base. The cardboard is cut 2 inches larger overall than the baseplate, then glued and stapled in place (photo 6). I give the armrest three layers of cardboard for extra strength.

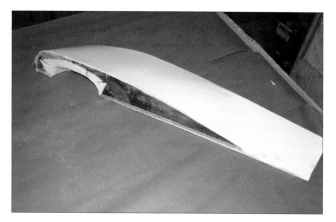

PHOTO 6: Cardboard is used to transition the top of the armrest into the baseplate. It will take at least three layers of cardboard to properly stiffen this armrest.

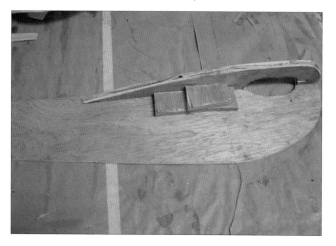

PHOTO 7: I stacked and glued plywood scraps under the top of the armrest to provide support and give me a very secure place to screw the armrest to the trim panel.

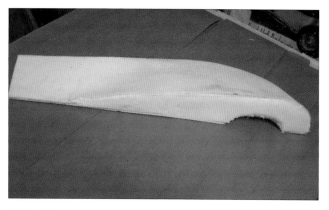

PHOTO 8: After spraying the cardboard-covered armrest with adhesive, the armrest gets a layer of ¼-inch-thick foam.

Here are some details that aren't so obvious. When attaching the top plate to the baseplate, I positioned the top plate ¼ inch below the top edge. This allows for the ¼-inch-thick foam padding I'll be adding to the top. I also stacked and glued two pieces of scrap ½-inch plywood under the top (photo 7). This will add support to the top as well as provide a very secure place to screw the armrest to the trim panel.

FOAM PADDING

The best foam padding for use when constructing automotive trim panels is ⅛- and ¼-inch-thick closed-cell foam. Both thicknesses come in 54-inch-wide rolls up to 30 yards long. Determining how much to buy depends on the size of the car being trimmed out and the complexity of the design. For example, I'll use ¼-inch-thick foam on the door, quarter panel trim panels, and roof side panels. That will give these panels a thicker, softer look. I'll need about 8 yards. I'll use ⅛-inch-thick foam padding to make the accent pieces such as the red bands on the side panels and the centerpiece for the roof panel. The thinner padding will allow these pieces to tuck neatly against the thicker foamed pieces for a very clean look. I won't need quite so much of this material; I'll order 6 yards. Knowing how much foam padding to order also tells me how much vinyl to order: 6 yards of light gray, 3 yards of dark gray, and 1 yard of red.

If there is anything to know about gluing closed-cell foam padding to the base panels and vinyl covering it is that the foam must be sanded to break the film on its surface. If this film isn't broken, it can easily separate from the padding beneath and ruin all of your hard work. I use 80-grit sandpaper to roughen up the foam surface and break the film.

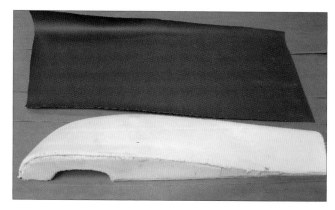

PHOTO 9: One of the tricks to covering an armrest is to align the vinyl material so that the stretch of the material goes lengthwise over the armrest.

Working on the armrest first, I begin by spraying both the foam piece and the armrest with 3M Super Trim Adhesive Yellow #8090. It's important to allow the adhesive to dry to the touch before covering the armrest. Once the adhesive dries, the armrest is then covered in foam (photo 8).

Adding the Vinyl

Next, I cut a piece of the dark gray vinyl that is slightly larger than the armrest (photo 9), then add adhesive to both the armrest and the back of the vinyl.

Here's a trick you can pick up only by watching the pros ply their craft. Cement the edge of the vinyl to the work bench; it's like gaining an extra hand when it comes to stretching the vinyl tightly over the armrest (photo 10). A lot of stretching and pulling is needed to get wrinkle-free results. By the way, vinyl has a grain that allows it to stretch more in one direction than in the other. Use that stretching action lengthwise on the armrest to get a glove-tight fit (photo 11).

Next comes the red insert. I start by cutting a length of lauan plywood to match the red insert I drew on the door template pattern. I cover the plywood with foam, then cover the foam with a strip of red vinyl (photo 12).

How did I secure the armrest and red-striped panel to the door trim panel? I gave both pieces a generous application of adhesive, then screwed and stapled both pieces

to the trim panel. The trick to stapling is in selecting staples that are the correct length, in this case ½-inch-long staples work best. I use 1-inch-long wood screws only in the area of the armrest, where I added the scrap plywood for support. Finally, both ends of the red stripe and the single end of the armrest are wrapped around the edges of the trim panel and secured with staples (photo 13).

The kick panels and the quarter panel trim panels are constructed using the same techniques used to make the

PHOTO 11: The final result is a very nice-looking armrest.

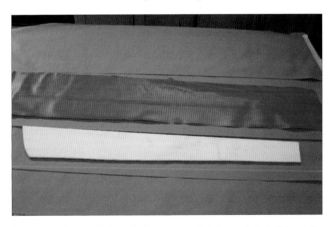

PHOTO 12: This accent piece will be covered with bright red vinyl. I'll leave the ends loose so that they can be wrapped over the edge of the trim panel once this piece is glued and stapled into place.

PHOTO 10: Another trick to covering an armrest is to staple one side of the cover to the bench.

PHOTO 13: The finished door panel. Notice that the wrapped ends of the insert and armrest give the panel a very professional look.

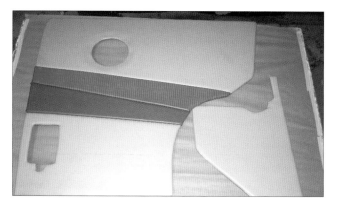

PHOTO 14: The quarter trim and kick panel are covered in the same light gray vinyl. Notice that the red stripe is continued onto the quarter panel trim.

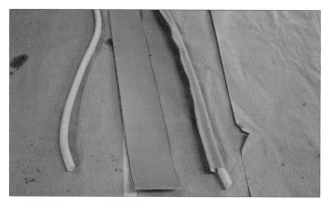

PHOTO 15: Wind lace is made by gluing and wrapping vinyl material around a soft rubber core. Gluing eliminates the need for sewing.

PHOTO 16: The new wind lace is stapled into place around the door opening, then screwed to the floor pan to make it more secure.

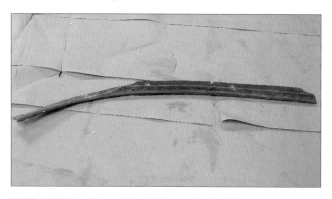

PHOTO 17: This headliner retainer strip is out of a Ford Pinto. It will work great over the door openings in the '46.

door trim panel, with a template and a little lauan plywood (photo 14). The problem is that I can't install either of these panels until I have the wind lace that wraps around the door openings mounted.

WIND LACE

In the old days, most cars used wind lace around the door openings to stop the wind, thus the name. It not only slowed the wind, it also improved on the looks of the interior. Since the overall fit of the car was poor, a little fabric overlap acted to hide a lot of sins.

To make the wind lace, I start by cutting two 2½-inch-wide strips from the roll of light gray vinyl. I'll need 10 feet per side, and since it is considered poor form to cut and sew pieces of vinyl together to make a wind lace, I'll cut my strips from along the outer edge of the roll.

The core of the wind lace is a ½-inch-thick round rubber material purchased from my local trim shop. All I have to do to make the end product is apply glue to the underside of the vinyl, let it dry, then wrap the vinyl around the rubber core (photo 15).

Since this car originally came with wind lace around the door openings, most of the retainer clips are already in place. Where the retainer clips are missing, I secured the wind lace to the opening using 1-inch staples. I also screwed the ends of the wind lace to the floor pan with #8 flat-head sheet metal screws just to be sure it remained secure (photo 16).

I still need a way to neatly tuck the headliner behind the wind lace at the top of the door opening. I opt to visit my local automotive reclamation center and scavenge the headliner retainer strips from two Ford Pintos (photo 17). These retainers will allow me to bring the headliner down and over the retainers, where I can tuck them under for a very nice look (photo 18).

PHOTO 18: The headliner is tucked beneath the retainer strip to give it a finished look.

NOTES

CHAPTER 20

HEADLINER AND
CENTER CONSOLE

Before any of the trim panels constructed previously can be mounted in the car, I need to install the headliner. The important thing to understand here is that the headliner that is going into the '46 is a custom-made headliner. It isn't like the headliner in your Toyota. It doesn't fall down after removing a few screws; once installed, it is in the car forever.

CONSTRUCTING THE FRAMEWORK

Take a look at photo 1. This is the completed framework for the new headliner. Eventually, this framework will be covered with a cardboard base and a layer of foam, then finished with a vinyl material to form the new headliner. Notice that the wires for the dome light have already been added. This is a very important step; once the headliner is complete, no additional wiring up here will be possible.

To make this framework, I start by cutting new headliner bows (photo 2). These are made of ½-inch thick plywood, cut about 2 inches wide, and have been shaped to fit the contour of the roof panel. Originally, these bows would have been made of metal rods and would have extended across the width of the roof at various intervals. The original headliner would have been attached to the rods, the same way curtains are attached to curtain rods, and stretched across the roof panel. My headliner will be glued and stapled into place using these wooden bows as support.

Referring back to photo 1, notice that I added ¼-inch-thick plywood strips lengthwise on the roof to help position and secure the cross bows. Also notice the square piece of ½-inch-thick plywood near the center of the roof. This is the mounting platform for the dome light. Finally, notice that I added additional ¼-inch-thick plywood strips around the back glass opening and between the quarter glass openings and the rear sail panel. Extra support is needed in these areas to provide attachment points for the cardboard base panels that will be added later. Everything you see here has either been glued and stapled together using 1-inch-long staples or screwed to the metal framework of the car using 1-inch #8 sheet metal screws.

The next step is to add more insulation. This is the same recycled foam rebond material I used to insulate the cowl area earlier. It is glued into place on the roof panel using 3M Super Trim Adhesive Yellow #8090 (photo 3).

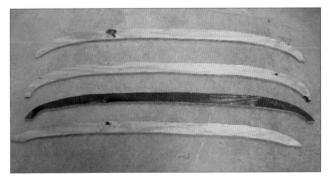

PHOTO 2: To make the framework, I start by cutting new headliner bows from ½-inch plywood.

PHOTO 1: The new headliner will be attached to this wooden framework.

PHOTO 3: Rebond insulation is added between each of the new roof bows.

BUILDING IN SECTIONS

Because I'm a novice at this, I'm not going to attempt to install a full headliner. Most fabrics and vinyl materials come in 54-inch-wide rolls, and I need about 80 inches to span the entire width of my roof. To accomplish that feat, I would need to sew two pieces of vinyl together.

To get around the need for sewing, I'll break this headliner into three separate sections: a left side, a right side, and a center section. The right and left sides will be

PHOTO 4: The center section is made of lauan plywood. Notice the hole for the dome light.

PHOTO 5: Notice that the layers of cardboard backing used to form the sides of the headliner stop at the edges of the insert and have been sanded smooth for a nice even surface.

PHOTO 6: The closed-cell foam padding is added next. Notice the sanding streaks visible on the surface of the foam.

covered with the light gray vinyl material, and the center section will be covered with the dark gray vinyl. The result will be a somewhat dramatic effect, and no one will ever suspect my inability to sew a straight line.

CENTER SECTION CONSTRUCTION

I start by making the center section. This is the only part of the headliner that will not be made in place on the roof. It will be a separate panel made out of lauan plywood and will extend the full length of the roof. Once the side panels are completed, it will be put into place and anchored to the roof using the same GM-style plastic retainers I used to attach the door and quarter trim panels.

To make the panel visually appealing, I make it 26 inches wide at the front and 20 inches wide at the rear (photo 4). That gives me a starting place, so the next step is to make the side panels.

SIDE PANEL CONSTRUCTION

To make the side panels, I use the same heavy cardboard I used previously to construct the templates for the door and quarter panel trim panels. I use the largest sheets possible and glue each one into place over my wooden framework until I have a base for the foam, which will be added next. This base needs to consist of at least three layers of cardboard to give it the needed strength to hold the foam and vinyl coverings.

To make the curves at the back of the roof, I cut the cardboard into smaller pieces and carefully sculpt the needed curves. I don't use any staples here because, once the sides have been covered and shaped, the cardboard will need to be sanded smooth using a dual-action sander with 80-grit sandpaper. Imperfections such as overlapped edges of the cardboard will telegraph through the foam and must be removed. The 80 grit will easily remove those edges (photo 5). As you can see in photo 5, I didn't bother to extend the cardboard to the center of the roof panel; most of this area will be covered by the center section.

Next up is the foam padding (photo 6). I'm using ¼-inch-thick closed-cell foam, and I'll glue it into place over the cardboard. To remove any wrinkles that form, especially in the corners, I pull the foam at the base of the wrinkle until it lies smooth. Any wrinkles that don't pull out can be sanded smooth using 80-grit sandpaper.

Notice in photo 6 that the foam is cut along a very straight line where this part of the headliner will eventually meet the center section. This straight line is essential to the overall look of the headliner and was drawn using the center section base panel as the pattern (photo 7).

The last step is to cover the side panels with vinyl material. I start by coating both the foam and the vinyl with adhesive. The adhesive is allowed to dry to the touch before attempting installation. Allowing the adhesive to partially dry is a very important step, as it will let me lightly stick the vinyl to the foam and reposition it, if needed, without worry of tearing the foam. Only after the vinyl is in place and wrinkle free do I press it firmly to the foam (photo 8).

I repeat this exercise on the left side, and then the roof is ready for the center section.

FINISHING THE CENTER SECTION

I've already constructed the base of the center section out of lauan plywood. All that is left to do is add the plastic push-in retainers, which you can see already in place in photo 7, cover them with a layer of ⅛-inch-thick foam, and cover that with the darker vinyl material. Why did I switch to the ⅛-inch-thick foam and not use the ¼-inch-thick foam? Using the thicker foam will make the edges of the center section stand proud of the side panels and create a shadowing effect. The thinner foam prevents that. How does the final product look? I think it looks great (photo 9).

THE CONSOLE AND CARPET

Carpet first, then console? Or is it the other way around? Actually it is both. I need at least some of the carpet installed before the console can be installed. But because the console will be built in place, I'd rather not have all of the carpet installed. Building the console in place requires a lot of crawling in and out of the car, a lot of wood splinters from the construction of the console, and errant drops of glue hitting here and there inside the car as I cover the console with the dark gray vinyl. This is no environment for pristine carpet. But then, I want to sit the console on top of a carpeted driveshaft tunnel. So that means some of the carpet must go down. I'll start by covering the floor pan with a layer of rebond padding.

As you move through the next few photographs, notice that the side trim panels are not in the car. Leaving them out will let me extend the floor pan carpet past the bottom edges of the panels, and that ensures that once the trim panels are installed the carpet will be tucked neatly beneath the trim panels with no gaps or exposed areas of the floor pan showing.

SOME CARPET AND PADDING

Needless to say, the floor pan must be clean and dry before adhering the rebond padding. Carpet takes a beating and must be securely anchored to the floor to prevent being torn, unraveled, or pulled up.

PHOTO 7: The center section is propped into place in order to mark the lines where the side panels will meet this panel. This line must be perfect so that it doesn't detract from the looks of the headliner.

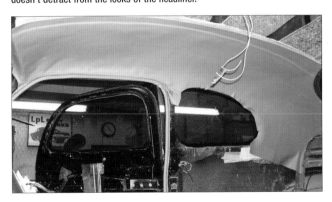

PHOTO 8: The foam is covered with the light gray vinyl. It takes time to get this right, so be prepared to look up for a while.

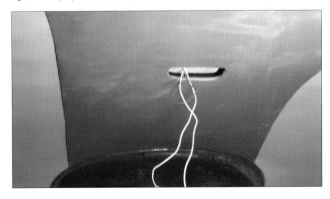

PHOTO 9: The completed headliner. The contrasting darker gray color of the center section makes this a striking addition to the car.

PHOTO 10: The rebond padding is adhered to the floor pan. Notice that I left an inch of space between the padding and the inside edge of the rocker panel. This will reduce the carpet thickness in this area for a cleaner look.

PHOTO 11: The first part of the floor pan to be carpeted is the driveshaft tunnel. This allows me to bring the floor pan carpeting to the edge of the tunnel and gives the carpet a seamless appearance.

PHOTO 12: The rear half of the console serves as an armrest for the rear seat passengers. Notice the cup holders and the power outlet.

The rebond padding is glued into place (photo 10). I'm still using 3M Super Trim Adhesive Yellow #8090. Notice that I didn't pad the driveshaft tunnel. No need for padding here, as the console will cover the bulk of the tunnel. Notice also that I left an inch of space between the rebond and the edges where the carpet will tuck under the side trim panels. This reduces the amount of material buildup that has to be forced beneath the side trim panels once they are installed. I left an inch of space along the sides of the driveshaft tunnel and around the seat mounting brackets as well, which allows me to cover these areas with scraps of carpet (photo 11). The floor pan carpet, once it is installed, can overlap this selvage edge for a clean look.

CONSOLE CONSTRUCTION

The plan calls for a console that extends the full length of the cab. It will start just underneath the center of the dash and work its way to the rear of the cab, where it will transition into a center armrest for the rear-seat passengers.

The console will also serve as a conduit for the wiring that leads to the rear of the car, and for that reason will become a permanent fixture inside the car. Once completed, the console will give the illusion of being two separate pieces: a front section and a rear section. That's because the rear section will be only half as wide as the front section.

As mentioned earlier, the rear section is basically an elongated armrest. I'll add a couple of cup holders for passenger convenience as well as a power outlet to plug in those digital gizmos kids can't seem to do without these days (photo 12).

The forward section is a little more complicated. Up here, I need the rear portion of the front section to be elevated to a height comfortable enough for the

PHOTO 13: The front half of the console is much wider and will house a storage compartment, cup holders, the shifter, and a stereo.

PHOTO 14: The base of the console. Notice the wire loom snaking through the bottom of the console and the cup holder holes cut into the framework.

PHOTO 15: The sides are stapled to the framework of the console and covered with foam and dark gray vinyl.

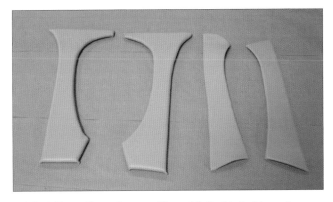

PHOTO 16: These pillar post covers will complete the interior trim work.

driver to use as an armrest. As measured from the floor pan, this height is 15 inches (photo 13).

The top of the forward armrest will be a flip-up door leading to a storage compartment below. I eliminated the glove box in the dash, so having someplace to store things like vehicle paperwork is very important.

I'll bring the front piece of the forward section up almost vertically and let it disappear just behind the face of the dash. This will be the perfect place to mount a stereo.

Console construction is very simple. I use a length of ½-inch-thick plywood to form the base, and then I build up each section using additional pieces of ½-inch-thick plywood mounted vertically on the base (photo 14).

The sides of the console are cut from a sheet of lauan plywood and stapled to the console frame. Once the sides are in place, they are covered with a layer of ¼-inch foam and the dark gray vinyl (photo 15). The top portions of the console are fabricated on the bench before being attached to the framework with the GM-style plastic push-in retainers. The result of all this work can be seen in photo 13. The design is pretty basic, but it is very functional.

FINISHING THE INTERIOR

A lot of hard work has already gone into fabricating the interior for the '46, so now it is time to start putting all of the pieces together. I'll start by taking care of some last-minute details.

The first of these last-minute details concerns the windshield and door pillar post covers. To make these panels, I cut matching pieces of lauan plywood, two for the windshield pillars and two for the door posts, and then I cover all four pieces with ⅛-inch-thick foam and the light gray vinyl (photo 16). A little silicone adhesive is used to hold them in place.

Next on the list are the sun visors. Luckily, I still have the frames of the old visors. I start by refinishing the frames with the same metallic gray paint I used to paint the dash. Then I trace the outline of the old visors onto

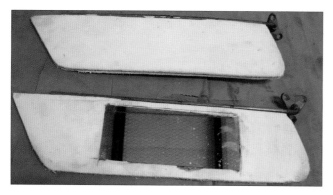

PHOTO 17: A mirror is glued to the old right-hand sun visor before it is covered with ⅛-inch-thick foam.

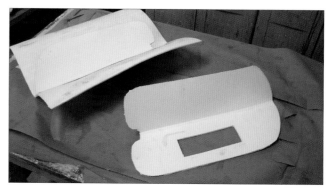

PHOTO 18: The new covers are covered with foam. Notice the opening for the mirror cut into the right-hand cover.

sheets of cardboard, adding an inch all around. The idea here is to have enough cardboard to sandwich over the old visor. Since passengers always need a mirror, I take an auto parts store mirror and glue it to the old visor. After the glue dries, I add ⅛-inch-thick foam to the remainder of the visor (photo 17). That gives me a flat, smooth surface to glue my new cardboard covers over the old visors.

To complete the new covers, I cut an opening for the mirror in the right-hand visor, then cover both covers with ⅛-inch-thick foam (photo 18). Finally, the new visor covers are covered with the light gray vinyl, then wrapped around the old visors. The result: a couple of very nice-looking visors (photo 19).

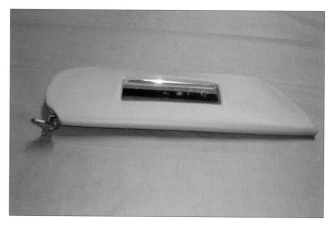

PHOTO 19: The end result is a very nice-looking visor.

FINISHING THE TRUNK

The trunk compartment gets basically the same treatment I gave the cab of the car. I start by making new side panels using the light gray vinyl, and then I cover the floor pan with carpet (photo 20). Notice in photo 20 that I added a Painless Performance battery cut-off switch (upper right rear corner). What's the hole in the right trim panel? I'll be adding a switch panel here that has a switch for the trunk light, a push button to open the driver's door, and an emergency switch to open the license plate pocket.

PHOTO 20: The trunk gets the same plush treatment I gave the interior.

NOTES

CHAPTER 21

THE
FINISHING TOUCHES

The time has come to put this ride on the ground. That means wheels and tires, and that means decisions about wheel styles and tire sizes. I could spend hours thumbing through catalog after catalog looking at everything from 14- to 20-inch-diameter wheels for this car. Have you seen the selections available? I have. If it is round, someone has designed it into a wheel.

My wheel selection will help me choose the tire style and size. You can't put a big fat tire on a skinny 20-inch-diameter wheel any more than you can put a skinny racing profile tire on a 14-inch-diameter wheel. The look just isn't there.

CHOOSING WHEEL SIZE AND TIRES

In the end, I decided to stay with the old-school look that has been prevalent throughout this build and went with American Racing Torq-Thrust D wheels (photo 1). I chose the 15-inch-diameter wheels that are 7 inches wide with gray painted spokes and a brushed aluminum rim.

How did I settle on 15-inch wheels that are 7 inches wide? The 15-inch-diameter wheel is the most common size out there, and since the theme of this car has been and still is old school, the choice came naturally. To determine the correct width, all I had to do was figure out the necessary tire clearance and wheel offset, and that left me with the correct wheel width.

PHOTO 1: These American Racing Torq-Thrust D gray spoke wheels are the perfect fit for this ride.

TIRE CLEARANCE

OK, there is a little more to it than that. The first step to determining wheel width is to determine the tire clearance. If you mount a fat radial tire on a 7-inch-wide wheel, you automatically have a total tire width of about 9 inches. I have 11 inches of rear wheel well space as measured from the inside edge of the rear fender to the inside of the wheel well. That's the space my wheel and tire will have to tuck into. Subtract 9 inches of tire width from the 11 inches of wheel well space, and I end up with about 1 inch of clearance on the inside and 1 inch of clearance on the outside. Thus the need for 7-inch-wide wheels.

OFFSET AND BACK SPACING

That's the easy part. The hard part starts when you pick up the phone to call the wheel guy and he asks about the desired wheel offset. What's wheel offset?

Offset is defined as the distance from the inside edge of the wheel to the mounting flange. In conjunction with offset, you will also hear the term *back spacing*. These are two different measurements but result in the same outcome as far as wheel widths are concerned.

Here is how it works. If a 7-inch-wide wheel has a back spacing of 3.5 inches (the distance from the mounting flange to the inside edge of the wheel), it also has an offset of zero. That means the mounting flange is centered in the wheel (7.0 - 3.5 = 3.5).

If a 7-inch-wide wheel has a back spacing of 2.5 inches, it also has an offset of negative 1.0 inch [7.0 – (2.5 + 1.0) = 3.5]. Negative offset simply means the mounting flange has been moved inboard, or closer to the inside edge of the wheel. A good example is a 7-inch-wide "deep dish" wheel. This wheel could have an offset of up to negative 5 inches. Positive offset is more like a wheel on a newer vehicle, where the wheel looks basically flat, and the mounting flange is located very near the outside edge of the wheel.

Applying the Concept

That's the definition of offset; now here is how to determine what offset works best for a particular application. I start by laying a straightedge vertically on the rear axle mounting flange, then measure the distance from the mounting flange to the inside edge of the fender wheel opening (photo 2). That measurement is 5½ inches.

A 7-inch-wide wheel with a zero offset has a measurement of 3.5 inches from the mounting flange to the outside edge of the wheel, plus roughly 1 more inch taking into consideration the width of the mounted tire, which leaves me with roughly 1 inch of clearance between the tire and the fender. That's not bad, but if you take a closer look at photo 2, you can see I've added a ½-inch wheel spacer to the axle for the purpose of doing some comparison work to see if adding more offset to the wheel would improve on the look. In the end, I elect to stick with 7-inch-wide wheels with a zero offset, and I hang the wheel spacers back on the wall.

You should also notice that I used the rear wheel well to make all of my calculations. Front wheel wells are always deeper and roomier to provide the needed clearance for turning, and therefore they don't lend themselves well to calculating wheel sizes and offsets. You should, however, test fit the wheel of choice on the front just to be sure no clearance problems exist.

As for tire selection, I'm going with BFGoodrich Radial T/A P215/65R15 tires on the front and BFGoodrich Radial T/A P225/70R15 tires on the rear. How does the car look with this wheel and tire combination (photo 3)?

CHECKING THE RIDE HEIGHT

Theoretically, the ride height for this car is perfect. It better be because I really don't have much of a choice when it comes to altering the ride height up front. That's OK, as I spent a lot of time working out the proposed ride height for this car back when I modified the frame. With the wheels and tires on the car, I can see my calculations were pretty close.

The rear suspension is a little more forgiving. Back here, I installed adjustable coil-over shock absorbers that allow me to increase the tension on the coil-over springs to push the rear of the car upward, or release a little tension on the springs to allow the rear of the car to drop. As the car now sits, I have a slight rake to the front, which I think is about perfect.

Let me warn you: get the ride height correct before delivering the car to the front end shop for an alignment. Even a slight change to the way the car sits can alter the setting on the front suspension. If you change the stance of the car after having the front end aligned, it is imperative that you have the front end realigned.

PHOTO 2: To determine where the axle mounting flange sits in relation to the fender, I measure the distance between the inside edge of the fender and the axle mounting flange; in this case, 6 inches.

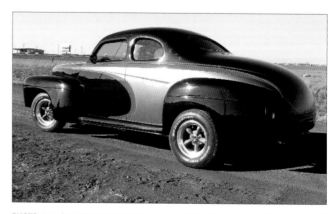

PHOTO 3: It is difficult to tell how a car will look with a particular tire and wheel combination until you move it out into the sunlight. I did, and I think this look is a winner.

FLUIDS AND BATTERY

Next for this ride are fluids (photo 4). The rear axle needs a quart of axle grease, the automatic transmission requires roughly 2 gallons of automatic transmission fluid (ATF), the engine needs 5 quarts of 10-30 motor oil, the power steering unit needs about 2 quarts of power steering fluid, the radiator needs 2 gallons of antifreeze, and the windshield washer tank needs 1 quart of washer fluid. To be certain the fuel gauge is working properly, I'll add at least 5 gallons of gasoline to the gas tank.

The next step is to power up the car. I did a thorough check of the electrical system as I progressed through the wiring phase of this ride, so everything in that department should be OK. All I need to add is a battery.

I actually have choices when it comes to batteries. I can go with the standard lead acid battery found in just about every Detroit creation out there, or I can go with the Optima brand battery. What's the difference? Without going into a lot of detail about how each of these batteries is constructed, I'll just say that when it comes to cars that are not driven on a daily basis and are subject to slow drains due to nonuse, the Optima battery outlasts the standard lead acid battery almost two to one.

STARTING UP

With the battery hooked up and all of the necessary fluids added to the car, it is time to bring out the Affordable Fuel Injection manual and go through the recommended start-up procedure. The best way to do this is to fold the manual open, climb into the driver's seat, and start reading.

Step one is to turn the ignition switch to the On position, and listen for the fuel pump to turn on for a few seconds then turn off. Turn the ignition switch to Off for at least ten seconds and repeat. The fuel pump should cycle and turn off.

Next, check the fuel system for leaks. If none are found, it is time to start the engine. The engine should start without having to depress the accelerator pedal. Let the engine run for a few minutes as you again check for fuel leaks.

Now it is time to set the timing. Turn the ignition switch to Off, and disconnect the single lead wire located behind the distributor. With this lead discon-

PHOTO 4: A lot of different fluids are required to keep a ride operating smoothly. Here I have oil, transmission fluid, power steering fluid, rear axle grease, and antifreeze. Don't forget the oil filter.

nected, restart the engine and set the timing to 0 degrees. Kill the engine, reconnect the lead, wait at least ten seconds, and restart the engine. If a code 42 shows up on the Check Engine light, disconnect the battery for at least one minute before restarting the engine. That should clear the computer of any codes.

At this point, the fuel injection system should take over the engine management and yield a lot of nice driving.

AIR CONDITIONING

Charging the Hot Rod Air air conditioning unit is not a do-it-yourself task. The system must be mechanically evacuated until a vacuum is created and held for at least an hour before adding the R134a refrigerant. The amount of R134a introduced into the system is also critical. This particular unit calls for exactly 1.8 pounds of R134a refrigerant. An undercharge of gas will result in insufficient cooling, while an overcharge of gas can damage the system.

It is also a good idea for the shop doing the work to introduce a leak-detecting charge to the system as it's being filled. Generally, a leak in the system is evident when the system initially refuses to vacuum down and hold that vacuum prior to the addition of R134a. On occasion, however, the leak is so slight that it takes several weeks before it's detectable. What's detectable? No more cold air out of the vents. A leak-detecting charge contains a dye that can be seen at the site of the leak no matter how slight the leak.

THE WALK AROUND

Before I take this ride out for its inaugural "get some thumbs up" spin, I thought I would take you for one last trip around the car. I showed you or told you about most of the proposed alterations made to this ride as I moved through this project. Other changes were so minor or last minute that I simply skimmed over them.

PHOTO 5: The chrome has been removed from the grille area, and everything up here has been painted.

PHOTO 6: The running boards were welded to the body, as were the rear fenders.

PHOTO 7: This detail, rounding off the upper corners of the deck, is easily missed since it blends so nicely into the flow of the car.

Starting at the front of the car, I discarded the front bumper to give the car a more streamlined look. I also did away with the chrome on the grille and added a narrow valance panel underneath the grille (photo 5).

On the sides of the car, I welded the running boards to the rocker panels and rear fenders. I think it cleaned up the look of the car by getting rid of a lot of body seams. I am particularly pleased with the outcome of welding the rear fenders to the body (photo 6).

Moving to the deck lid, I opted to round off all four corners of the lid. This is a very rounded car, and it just didn't seem right to leave the squared-off corners, especially the top two corners, of the deck lid (photo 7).

At the rear of the car, I spent quite a bit of time hacking, chopping, and welding in search of the perfect hidden license plate housing. In the end, I think this flip-down door really completes the look (photo 8).

This is something I spent a lot of time working out: recessing the taillights. The results speak for themselves (photo 9).

Opening the door to look inside the car, I decided to move away from the considered norm of painting the dash the same color as the exterior of the car. Instead, I painted the dash a silver metallic color to complement the gray interior and gave it a red stripe for the sole purpose of bringing the outside in. I think it worked out pretty well (photo 10).

FINAL NOTES

I could talk on and on about what I did to this car, the changes I made during the process of building this car, and whether the end result is worth all of the effort I put

PHOTO 8: This flip-down door on the rear valance panel hides the rear license plate when the car is parked.

PHOTO 9: The recessed taillights really add to the final touches of the car.

PHOTO 10: The red stripe added to the dash continues to flow around the car.

into it. Instead, I think I'll discuss the most important factors of a build like this: time, money, and budget.

TIME

I never enter into a project this size with a written-in-stone timeline. I do know from experience roughly how long a complete rebuild such as this is going to take. But if that time frame comes and goes and the car isn't finished, I don't go into a panic. A build like this takes as long as it takes.

We have a saying in this business that goes something like this: never enough time to do it right, but always enough time to do it over. Doing it over means spending more money, and if there is one thing I hate it is spending the same money twice. Fortunately, most garage restorers/garage car builders aren't on a time schedule. That should equate to slowing down and doing it right the first time.

Let me clarify that statement: I take the time it takes to do a job right. But in my world, doing it right may mean taking a hammer to all the hard work just completed because I'm not happy with the result. It isn't that I've done a lousy job, it is just that I don't like the result. I have no problem with trashing weeks of work just so I can try something else that in the end may be a vast improvement over what I originally had in mind. So the bottom line is not to worry about the schedule; worry about the end result and get it right for the car being built.

Are you curious about how long it took? I spent roughly four hours a day, five days a week for almost two years working on this car. You can calculate the total if desired while I go on to the budgetary aspects of a build like this.

MONEY AND BUDGETING

I won't disclose how much money was spent on this build, but I can tell you that I know the amount right down to the last penny. Is the car worth the amount of money I spent building it? Yes, without a doubt—which reminds me of another saying we have in this business: If you spend $5,000 on a $500 car, you still have a $500 car. This saying is well worth remembering if you are considering pouring money into a car only you will love. And that brings me to budgeting.

I can't tell you how many people I've talked to over the years who thought they could restore an old car or build a hot rod for a few hundred bucks. They seem almost shocked when I tell them the job they are considering will actually cost in the five-figure range, if not a lot more. What that tells me is that they never bothered to work out a cost budget, which is the easiest thing in the world to do, especially after the invention of the PC.

Most home computers come equipped with some form of spreadsheet software. What's a spreadsheet? It is little more than a page filled with limitless rows and columns, each one of which can be summed and totaled to your heart's desire. Part names can be listed, part sources can be listed, and part prices can be listed. I even go so far as to make a column listing the estimated costs. That gives me a proposed budget before I ever even turn a wrench and lets me continually compare my actual spending with my estimated spending. You'll be surprised how thrilled you can become seeing the actual cost of a build hovering below the estimated cost. This is a wife-pleasing moment.

What parts should be listed on the spreadsheet? I list every conceivable part the car will ever need. I'm talking about everything, including the price of solder for making wire connections and the cost of hand soap for cleaning up before supper. Yes, I know listing parts can be a daunting task, but list everything you can think of, and don't hesitate to add rows to the spreadsheet as you move deeper into the project and find that there are more parts that you need.

Once the initial parts list is complete, I browse catalogs, Internet sites, and even call my local parts store for prices. Each part is priced and the source is named. Six months later when I need a pair of power window regulators, it helps to know where I got the price listed on the spread sheet.

One thing I don't do is calculate the cost of labor into the budget. I don't have to as I do 95 percent of the labor myself, and my labor rate varies depending on my attitude on a given day. The remaining 5 percent of the labor cost is rolled into the cost of the part. A good example is engine work. Engine parts cost only so much. It is the labor to make all those parts work correctly that drive the cost of a good engine through the roof.

As work on the project begins, the actual cost of the parts being purchased is listed in a separate column next to the estimated cost column. That lets me know if I've found a good deal or if I've blown the budget in a particular area. Speaking of good deals, I never pass up the opportunity to browse eBay for a good deal. People are always changing their minds when it comes to car building. Someone may have purchased the exact part you need but later decided to go another route. You may get that part on eBay for a song.

YOUR RIDE

So whether your next project car still has weeds growing around it or has been collecting dust in the garage for the past few years, this book will help put your project back on track. Old cars like the '46 return to the road only when someone like you takes the time to put them there. So do a reread, dog-ear a few pages, and go to work. I hate touring the city alone. See you on the road.

NOTES

NOTES

Appendix

SUPPLIERS

Affordable Fuel Injection
9415 W. Ridge Rd.
Elsie, MI 48831
248-431-1772
www.affordable-fuel-injection.com
Fuel injection systems for street rods

American Racing Custom Wheels
19067 S. Reyes Ave.
Rancho Dominguez, CA 90221
310-635-7806
www.americanracing.com
Chrome wheels

The Hoffman Group
201 SE Oak St.
Portland, OR 97214
800-651-1970
www.thehoffmangroup.com/autoloc/
Door latches, power window units, and door hinges

Auto Meter
413 West Elm St.
Sycamore, IL 60178
866-248-6356
www.autometer.com
Street rod instrument gauges

Crest Industries
231 Larken Williams Industrial Court
Fenton, MO 63026
800-733-2737
www.crestmidwest.com
Automotive molding clips and fasteners

The Eastwood Company
263 Shoemaker Rd.
Pottstown, PA 19464
800-343-9353
www.eastwoodco.com
Automotive tools and supplies

Flaming River
800 Poertner Dr.
Berea, OH 44017
800-648-8022
www.flamingriver.com
Street rod steering columns

Gerald's Aussie Auto Glass
4001 Canyon Dr.
Amarillo, TX 79110
806-354-0422
www.aussieglass.com
Street rod glass and windshields

Hot Rod Air
9330 Corporate Dr.
Suite 308
Selma, TX 78154
877-693-3200
www.hotrodair.com
Street rod and vintage car air conditioning systems

House of Kolor
210 Crosby St.
Picayune, MS 39466
601-798-4229
www.houseofkolor.com
Automotive refinishing products

LizardSkin LLC
405 Madison Ave.
Suite 1550
Toledo, OH 43604
877-278-9468
www.lizardskin.com
Automotive undercoating and sound-deadening products

LPL Body Works
5815 Contented Lane
Amarillo, TX 79109
806-359-9783
www.lplbodyworks.com
Automotive restoration experts

Painless Performance Products
2501 Ludelle St.
Fort Worth, TX 76105
817-244-6212
www.painlessperformance.com
Automotive wiring products

Steele Rubber Products
6180 E. NC 150 Hwy
Denver, NC 28037
800-447-0849
www.steelerubber.com
Automotive weatherstripping products

Wilwood Engineering
4700 Calle Bolero
Camarillo, CA 93012
805-388-1188
www.wilwood.com
Street rod braking systems

Index